A BETTER HUMAN

THE STOIC HEART, MIND, AND SOUL

By George J. Bradley

BP

Bradley Publishing Inc.
New York, NY

ISBN 978-0-692-90492-3
Bradley, George J. (June 2017).
A Better Human: The Stoic Heart, Mind, and Soul.
Bradley Publishing. Paperback Edition.

TO MY WIFE, YULIA

"IT IS THE POWER OF THE MIND TO BE UNCONQUERABLE." - SENECA

Part I: Heart

Part II: Mind

Part III: Soul

Introduction

We all want to be good.

Scratch that. We all want to be great. We want to be the very best we can be. It's like that old advertising jingle from the U.S. Army: Be All That You Can Be.

But how?

Of all the religions, creeds, and self-help manifestos the world has produced, most concentrate on how to achieve salvation in another aspect, with our lives merely transitory testing grounds for a higher realm. Or they provide prescriptions for how to limit human impact on the world and its suffering. Or we pursue "enlightened hedonism" and try to balance our own consumption, as a goal in and of itself, with an ever-shrinking pool of worldly resources.

This is all well and good, if these are your desires.

But what if you are striving to be great? How do you do that? What is greatness and why achieve it?

With the possible exception of certain schools of Buddhism, most systems of thought aim only to teach people how to live well in this world as a by-product of a larger moralistic program. We should be good to our neighbors, treat them as we would have them treat us. We should not kill. We should not steal. In more severe models, we should not eat certain foods or harm other creatures whenever possible. We should do these things because "god" or "God" or "gods" decreed it to be so. Or, if we don't believe in God(s), we should apply enlightened rationale to our behavior and . . . none of this teaches how to be better humans now, in this life, or how to be the best humans we can possibly be.

But one group of thinkers did lay out a prescription for how to lead a life that produces success and enjoyment of life in the here and now.

They've gotten a bad rap for this over the ages, undeservedly so.

We're going to talk about them in this book because the ideas – and not just the ideas but the actual practices – they developed are not only relevant to modern life, but are the key, still, now, to success and fulfillment.

This is a philosophy called Stoicism.

It's founder was a man named Zeno of Citium who, in 3rd Century BC Athens, led a somewhat itinerant discussion group, or 'school' much like those of the more famous philosophers Socrates, Plato, and Aristotle.

The philosophy developed through a succession of Greek teachers and thinkers but really blossomed in Rome. There, famous leaders like Cicero and Cato the Younger took up the lifestyle and used it to shape not only their outlook on life but also the success of their careers and their ability to weather the stresses and changes of a world changing from democracy to Empire.

Yet the three most influential Stoic thinkers (and practitioners) were still to come: Seneca (an advisor to Emperor Nero and an extremely successful businessman in his own right); Epictetus (a freed Greek slave who did very well as a teacher in Rome); and the "Good Emperor" Marcus Aurelius, whose Meditations are a personal daybook of private Stoic thoughts that have been read and cherished by millions facing similar leadership and life challenges throughout the ages.

Our book, the one you're now reading, will draw heavily on the thinking and writing of these three practical philosophers. It will link their teaching and their ways of living and thinking to our modern times. And it will build upon some other notable modern-day works that also touch on Stoicism and have, in combination, worked to give Stoicism a rebirth in popular thought and culture. These works include Ryan Holiday's Obstacle is the Way, William Irvine's A Guide to the Good Life, Robert Greene and 50 Cent's awesome collaboration The 50th Law, and Angela Duckworth's study about perseverance and hard work, which is aptly named Grit.

Before we begin with the material, which explores Stoicism in a step-by-step process to give you first the basics – the Heart of how to live a Stoic life; and then the refinement – or Mind; followed up by some deeper touchstones – our Soul section; before we go there I'd like to share just one small anecdote. I'd like you to read this because it shows what an amazing transformative power Stoicism can have in your life, what a roadmap to greatness in heart, mind, and soul it offers. It's a roadmap that has been carefully laid out, but forgotten. Or maligned. Applying the tenets of stoicism, often associated incorrectly with dourness and a disdain for earthly enjoyment and sociability, will not only create joy but set definitions for what greatness is and stepping stones for how to reach it. It will do this for you in the best of times and in the worst. It applies equally to the mundane tasks of daily life and to the most arduous, most trying, most soul wrenching. Such as this experience, related by the modern Stoic, former Vice Presidential Candidate, and long-time Prisoner of War, Admiral John Stockdale. He talks about how important his newfound Stoic philosophy was to him, and he credits it with keeping him alive and sane during his long imprisonment. The whole article is certainly a moving, necessary read, but I'll restrict myself to just this paragraph since I simply want to light a fire in you, a thirst, for the same type of steadfast excellence that Stockdale's Stoic lifestyle helped him develop:

> Fear was not something that came out of the shadows at night and enveloped you; he [Epictetus] charged you with the total responsibility of starting it, stopping it, controlling it. This was one of Stoicism's biggest demands on a person. Stoics can be made to sound like lazy brutes when they are described merely as people indifferent to most everything but good and evil, people who make stingy use of emotions like pity and sympathy. But add this requirement of total personal responsibility for each and every one of your emotions, and you're talking about a person with his hands full. I whispered a "chant" to myself as I was marched at gunpoint to my daily interrogation: "control fear, control guilt, control fear, control guilt." And I devised methods of deflecting my gaze to obscure such fear and guilt as doubtless emerged in my eyes when I temporarily lost control under questioning. You could be bashed for failure to look at the face of your interrogator; I concentrated on his left earlobe, and he seemed to get used to it – thought I was a little cockeyed, probably. Controlling your emotions is difficult but can be empowering. Epictetus: "For it is within you, that both your destruction and deliverance lie."[i]

While I'm not saying that you, reader, will have as much need for this type of empowerment and this type of self-control — hopefully never having to be a prisoner-of-war yourself — I am saying that the principles Stockdale and so many others have used so effectively apply equally well in the normal world.

I've treaded this road myself.

I've experienced the benefits.

And, through a combination of original selections from the Stoic masters, anecdotes from life and pop culture of our modern world, and my own more normal experiences, I think you'll come away not only convinced but also enthused about the journey of success and enjoyment Stoicism can offer for your own life.

PART I: Heart

CHAPTER 1
Building Awareness of What Is and Isn't in Your Control

According to the ancient program outlined by Stoic thinkers, one of the first and most essential building blocks for becoming a better human being is to develop an awareness of what is and isn't in your power to control.

Epictetus defines the basics of this when he says,

> Of things some are in our power, and others are not. In our power are opinion, movement toward a thing, desire, aversion (turning from a thing); and in a word, whatever are our own acts: not in our power are the body, property, reputation, offices (magisterial power), and in a word, whatever are not our own acts. And the things in our power are by nature free, not subject to restraint nor hindrance: but the things not in our power are weak, slavish, subject to restraint, in the power of others.[ii]

The doctrine laid out here is simple. It is simple to understand. But it requires a different mindset. And it produces a different outcome.

The mindset asks you to stop and think. It demands you make rational choices and do so not according to a complicated set of laws or a shifting sense of what is acceptable in a social or moral hierarchy but according to one rule only: do you truly control the issue? This requires simple but honest evaluation of a circumstance to determine whether it is something you, personally, can affect. If not, the circumstance is not controllable and should not – even *cannot*, according to absolute stoic thinking – be a cause for concern. If it is controllable, then the increased focus you can bring to bear because you've put aside all the other uncontrollable issues will allow you, via techniques discussed in later chapters such as hard work, perseverance, and agility, to make astounding strides. You'll overcome obstacles as if they were not obstacles, not as if they don't exist but as if they have become essential building blocks to success.

Epictetus goes on to say, "You can be invincible, if you enter into no contest in which it is not in your power to conquer. Take care then . . . to despise the things which are not in our power."iii

This process speaks to achievement. It speaks to self-improvement. It helps, as we'll soon see, to direct effort and thought and willpower toward problems where such effort, thought, and willpower will matter. But additionally, and intentionally − rather than as an unintentional byproduct like in most other systems of thought − this process leads toward virtue, a sense of worldly fulfillment and even joy, and a prescription on how best to live life now, here, in this world, so as not to someday look back on our lives and be forced to admit to ourselves that we've mislived.

The tenets of Stoicism, its results, and a few tricks and techniques for encouraging a Stoic mindset will occupy a large part of the remainder of this book. But, right now we need to better understand the principle of rational decision-making based on what is and what isn't controllable.

First, as William Irvine points out in his book "A Guide to the Good Life," Epictetus' division of all things into the categories of "things in our power" and "things not in our power" is ambiguous, especially the last part of the formula.[iv] It could be very black and white: there are some things we just cannot ever control. Or it could mean that there are things over which we have some, but not full control. Or his statement could really mean both, in which case we have what Irvine proposes as a three-part formula:

1. Things over which we have control.
2. Things over which we have some, but not complete, control.
3. Things over which we have no control at all.

Epictetus provides lists for the first and third of these categories. For the first, he cites **opinion, movement toward a thing, desire,** and **aversion** (movement from a thing) as those we control. For the last category, he cites the **body, property, reputation,** and **offices** (magisterial power) as those over which we have no control. These are not all-inclusive lists of course. But neither do they take into account the middle category, things over which we have some, but not complete control.

An example of this might be a career.

We have control over some facets of our career choices. For instance, if we want to be a doctor or a lawyer or a pilot, we can take appropriate courses. We can study diligently to achieve the required grades. We can develop relationships with people who might serve as mentors. We can even take potential obstacles and turn them to our advantage, such as when the all-female crew of a Royal Brunei commercial jet landed in Saudi Arabia, where the women who piloted it cannot even drive a car. Captain Sharifah Czarena said, "It's really showing the younger generation or the girls especially that whatever they dream of, they can achieve it."[v] This is an example of how an obstacle to their career path (and other young women) has actually become a step on the road to success, a larger sort of success than just piloting an aircraft.

In the pursuit of achieving an objective, such as a career as a pilot, these things are under the control of you, as a human: your effort, your diligence, your work at forming connections and networking, and your ability to overcome and turn obstacles to your advantage.

But some things just might not be controllable.

Amy Purdy is a good example of this.

After bacterial meningitis led to her losing both her legs, she struggled with depression.

She was restricted from doing certain things. They were literally out of her control. She could not walk, dance, or participate in a lot of sports.

This restriction, or at least the absence of legs, falls into the third category of what we'll call Epictetus' revised equation. It's outside of personal control. Amy Purdy could not regrow legs in order to do the things she wanted to do.

But, instead, she focused on what she could control: using − even inventing − prosthetics that expanded her ability to participate and excel in the sports she loved. She built her own snowboarding prosthetics when suitable ones weren't yet available, became a world champion female adaptive snowboarder, and then a crowd favorite on dancing with the stars.[vi]

Instead of focusing on the limitation that was out of her control, and that would lead to nothing more than frustration and continuing depression, Amy Purdy directed her efforts and creativity to those things she could control. This led to tremendous success.

What Epictetus and other Stoic philosophers tell us to do is to focus on those things we can control. Be prepared to think about challenges differently. Spend energy on those things you're able to affect so that you put yourself in position to succeed. And if the rules or limitations prevent you from doing something, then consider being the person who changes the rules.

This leads us to the most amazing side effect of not sweating the things you can't control: **therein lies joy**.

The Stoics refer to this joy as tranquility (sounds Buddhist, doesn't it?)

The tranquility is not a silence, or an isolation. It's participation in the world. It is recognizing and tackling the issues under our control. As we do this, we move into a zone where we realize we can confront and overcome the problems we face, or that the problems we face — if truly out of our control — do not matter.

Irvine captures the process of arriving at Stoical joy and tranquility nicely when he writes:

> We will find ourselves experiencing fewer negative emotions. We will also find that we are spending less time than we used to wishing things could be different and more time enjoying things as they are. We will find, more generally, that we are experiencing a degree of tranquility that our life previously lacked. We might also discover, perhaps to our amazement, that our practice of Stoicism has made us susceptible to little outbursts of joy: We

will, out of the blue, feel delighted to be the person we are, living the life we are living, in the universe we happen to inhabit.[vii]

Now, before looking at this as a panacea for every ill, we need to mention that some things out of our control are also, at least from a hedonistic standpoint, not very good. To these the Stoics apply a ruthless sort of logic that will take time to fully absorb, if you decide to pursue the many benefits of a Stoical mindset. Yet, in the end, even the outcomes of such issues fit within the rational matrix of Epictetus' revised equation.

For instance, if a person lives in a time of famine or of severe drought, acquiring food or water might not actually be possible. Think, perhaps, of being shipwrecked on a desert isle. No food. No fresh water. You are faced with imminent and unavoidable death (many people in famine, even though not on an actual island, are in this very predicament). There is no measure of hard work, agility, perseverance, or ingenuity that will rescue you. Only luck or providence can assist, both of which are uncontrollable. More likely, though, the result will be death. Unpleasant for sure. But not, by any means, irrational.

As Seneca (and many other Stoic philosophers) have said, the only recourse is a brutal but rationally honest view of the situation:

> Reflect that no evils afflict one who has died, that the accounts which make the underworld a place of terror to us are mere tales, that no darkness threatens the dead, no prison, or rivers blazing with fire, no river of Forgetfulness, or seats of judgment, no sinners answering for their crimes, or tyrants a second time in that freedom which so lacks fetters: these are the imaginings of poets, who have tormented us with groundless fears. Death is a release from all pains, and a boundary beyond which our sufferings cannot go; it returns us to that state of peacefulness in which we lay before we were born. If someone pities those who have died, let him pity also those who have not been born. Death is neither a good nor an evil; for only that which is something can be a good or an evil; but what is itself nothing and reduces everything to nothingness, delivers us to no category of fortune.[viii]

This is the approach Stoics take to all issues – **all issues** – deemed beyond their personal control. No suffering actually attaches to such things. Or, if suffering does attach to it, that suffering is an effect of our minds and not of reality. So we choose to suffer or not to suffer in each case. Our level of control and our choices therein dictate our suffering: either we control a situation fully, or we do not control it. When we do not control it, perhaps it is a case where we control parts of the situation. Then we should – we must – direct our talents and efforts against those parts. In applying ourselves to things we control, we do our best and have no cause to suffer. If we do not control a situation, even if, or especially if, that situation is death, then we need not worry. The worry has no effect. And the end is rational.

A clever description of how to parse the issue of control comes from the Buddhist tradition, where a monk in the Himalayas became famous for his special knowledge and talents.[ix] He would journey to the local village on occasion and display these talents, one of which was to describe for the villagers the contents of their pockets, their safes, or even their thoughts.

One day a boy decided to play a joke on the monk and prove to his friends that the monk was a phony. He devised a plan. He captured a small bird and determined to hide it in his hands.

He knew, of course, that the monk would know it was a bird.

So he'd ask a follow-up question: was the bird dead or alive. If the monk said the bird was alive, the boy would crush it. If the monk said the bird was dead, the boy would open his hands and let the bird fly away.

No matter what the monk said, the boy could choose the other option and prove the monk to be a fraud.

When the monk next came down the mountain and into the village the boy walked up to him and said, "Old man, old man, what do I have in my hands?"

"You have a bird, my son." And he was right.

The boy then asked, "Is the bird alive, or is it dead?"

The wise old monk thought for a moment and then said, "It is as you choose it to be."

There are some things over which we have choice. And others where we either have only partial choice or no choice at all. It is up to us to apply our rational minds in making the distinction between these categories; our success as well as our tranquility and joy depends largely on our ability to do so.

Ryan Holiday provides another, perhaps more inclusive list of things in and out of our control in his book "The Obstacle is the Way." He says:

> And what is up to us?
>
> Our emotions
> Our judgments
> Our creativity
> Our attitude
> Our perspective
> Our desires
> Our decisions
> Our determination
>
> All the other things, the weather, the economy, circumstances, other people's emotions or judgments, trends, disasters, et cetera . . . every

ounce of energy directed at things we can't actually influence is wasted – self-indulgent and self-destructive. So much power – ours, and other people's – is frittered away in this manner.[x]

Practicing awareness of what is and what isn't in your control also helps dive deeper into the other techniques and benefits of Stoicism. It all goes back to what Holiday says above. If we haven't accurately determined whether an issue is fully or partially within our ability to influence, then bringing the Stoical techniques of agility, hard work, perseverance, creativity, mentorship, or perspective on past, future, and social fun to bear on a problem is as likely to be frittered away as successful. All of these things are good, in and of themselves. But directed at issues we can influence, they become great. They work in concert to produce, not in some hypothetical genius, but in you, you and me and the guy next door (if he's practicing a Stoic way of life), success, achievement, and joy. A life well-lived.

This principle applies not just to the beginning stages of a project or plan, but also to higher levels of achievement.

In his book "Executive Warfare" David D'Alessandro explains: "With a move into higher management, however, you're suddenly thrust into a new role, one where you are now managing experts in fields you have no knowledge of. It's a case of the blind leading the sighted, and if that role fails to alarm you, you're either too full of yourself, too immature, or just too plain stupid to be successful."[xi]

Knowing what you have control over is a development of rationality and of self-awareness. Being able to work in an environment where you don't control everything – where you can't control everything – where you are not the expert but have to rely on and manage those who are: that is what higher level management requires.

Without developing an awareness of and appreciation for how to work with, through, and even around the difficulties (and opportunities) or our ability to control situations and events, we waste time, we lead others poorly, and we close doors to creativity and agility. With that ability firmly in hand, doors open, new doors are created where only walls had been, and even as we work hard we do so in a tranquility of the sort that does not depend on fate or the will and whim of others.

CHAPTER 2
Self-Discipline

I'm from New Jersey.

For better or for worse, one thing we New Jersey-
ans are known for: road rage.

I haven't been immune from that.

In fact, one particular day a guy cut me off. I was
so mad that I pulled up beside him at the next light,
me in the left lane, him in the right. He was going
straight. So when the light changed I cut over hard
and crossed in front of him, getting my revenge by
forcing him to slam on his brakes as I whipped past
him.

I thought I taught him a lesson.

But, no. True to the Jersey spirit, my actions only
kindled my adversary's own road rage. It was like we'd
gotten ourselves into a death spiral, neither one of us
able to let go. He followed me all across town, yelling
at me, chasing me, doing crazy things. I started to

actually get worried that I'd picked on a bona fide psychopath. In the end I had to basically trick the guy. I turned down a street he didn't see and then doubled-back, losing him.

Whew.

Since then, I've examined myself (and I've also begun practicing a Stoic mindset in most things I do). And I've never again allowed myself to give into road rage. How have I managed such a change? How have I escaped something as integral to my nature and my upbringing as this sort of New Jersey driving habit?

Self-discipline.

That man had made a decision to cut me off. I had no control over his decision; totally nothing I could or should worry about. But I also made a decision myself in choosing to react the way I did. What that crazy driver did in the first place, though irritating, had no effect on me. But my decision in response – a thing I controlled almost completely – certainly affected me and could have affected me much worse if I hadn't been crafty enough to elude him and thus escape his retribution.

Though this story illustrates one reason why a Stoic's self-discipline is important, there are actually many benefits. William Irvine sums these up by saying, "those who possess [self-discipline] have the ability to determine what they do with their life. Those who lack self-discipline will have the path they take through life determined by someone or something else, and as a result, there is a very real danger they will mislive."[xii]

Implied in this statement, again, is the ability to discern what is and isn't under our control – the subject of the first chapter. The idea is to be disciplined and to do so in those areas – like choosing not to react to someone else's bad decision – where we have control. We must recognize where we have control **and then be disciplined** in those areas in terms of our own, controllable, actions.

In other words, neither you nor I can even start trying to be disciplined about things in that third category of Epictetus' formula. It's irrational to try to discipline yourself *not to die*. It's irrational to try to discipline yourself to flap your arms fast enough that you fly.

Those things (and many more) are out of our control. But it's not irrational to control parts of uncontrollable situations, like how we react in times of crisis, gloom, despair, or even times of triumph and joy.

These two things combine to produce self-discipline: knowing what we can control, then controlling what we can.

But how can we begin to develop self-discipline?

The Stoics offer several fascinating techniques that are not only practical but also, it turns out, tend to be supported more-and-more by science.

I won't cover every Stoic technique for self-discipline, but I will focus on what I'll call the "Big Five":

1. Negative visualization
2. Self-reflection
3. Practicing poverty
4. Faking positivity
5. Forgiving yourself

Let's briefly cover each of these.

Although it at first seems counterintuitive, one way to build self-discipline and help yourself endure or push through difficult situations is to force yourself to really imagine the worst possible outcome. Often, on close inspection, the very worst that could happen isn't actually all that bad.

Think about my road rage story. If I had just swallowed my pride and disciplined myself not to react to the man when he first cut me off, what was the worst thing that could have come from it? He'd already passed me. I was in no danger. In fact, I made the situation worse (potentially much worse) by reacting. Anxieties or fears we might bring to a situation can, on close inspection, often quickly be dismissed as exaggerated or untrue. Maybe I was worried that I'd lose face if I let someone cut me off. Maybe I was concerned that if I didn't teach that jerk a lesson he'd cause an accident at some point. Truthfully I don't know exactly what I was thinking when I reacted. I don't know what my exact rationale was for such a reaction. But if I had just made myself pause, and visualize the worst possible outcome from him cutting me off I would have realized there was none. None at all.

Self-reflection, the next Stoic technique for increasing self-discipline, is closely related to negative visualization. The difference between it and negative visualization is that self-reflection applies more to the scope or scale of the situation than to the repercussions. As Marcus Aurelius, the famous Stoic Emperor of Rome, wrote in his private diary: "the value of attentiveness varies in proportion to its object. You're better off not giving the small things more time than they deserve."[xiii]

In our day and age of instant communications, this advice hits the mark. Stop to reflect on the importance of, say, watching the latest cat videos that invade our Facebook pages (or taunting the internet troll who comments on our threads, or watching skate boarding tricks, whatever your jam is). The relative importance of such things, stacked up against other tasks, will pale. A few short moments of reflection in moments like this, weighing the benefits of one activity over the other, will reduce clutter in your life, free up time, and make self-discipline so much easier. Without pausing now and again for reflection, the little things in life tend to pile up so that we only ever glancingly deal with our bigger, more important tasks.

Tim Ferris, best-selling author of numerous self-help and inspirational books, bases many of his recommendations on Stoicism. He has done much to popularize the third Stoic technique for increasing self-discipline: the practice of poverty.

Ferris advocates regularly spending a few days at a time to take negative visualization to the next logical step: actually subjecting yourself to part of the 'worst case scenario.' Do away with fancy clothes, fancy meals, and fancy entertainment for a week. Live on fifty dollars. The benefits are enormous: you will forget your fear of scarcity, you'll feel a subtle but warming gratefulness for the things you do possess, you'll realize that luxury items are not essential to survival or even to enjoying life, and you'll save money too![xiv]

In addition, as Seneca warns, "Intense pleasures, when captured by us, become our captors, meaning that the more pleasures a man captures, 'the more masters he will have to serve.'"[xv] By periodically putting pleasures aside, we not only increase our enjoyment of them and gratitude for them when they are present, we also reduce both our fear of losing those pleasures and the hold that those pleasures have on our decision-making.

The fourth technique, faking positivity, seems shallow at first but is supported by hard science. Researchers studied more than 26,000 people, giving them different tasks and putting them in different situations. Those who were simply told to smile during a bad situation came out on top of **all other** techniques in terms of reporting how much happiness improved.[xvi]

As Seneca said, "Turn all [anger's] indications into their opposites."[xvii] These indications, of course, can be expanded beyond just forced smiling. Walk happily, instead of slouching. Make your voice more pleasant. Hold your head high. Look people in the eyes. All of these things work to create positivity – not imagined positivity but real emotions and reactions from other people too. And the act of forcing positive outward expressions conditions the body and the mind to experience joy. That conditioning process is a step along the road toward self-discipline. It hurts sometimes, choking back anger and replacing it with a facsimile of happiness, but in the end it allows you to look at everything with real, rather than metaphorical, rose-tinted glasses.

Just think what might have happened if, instead of plotting my revenge against the guy who cut me off I instead pleasantly waved at him and smiled. (Well, my friends might have revoked my New Jersey driver's license for such behavior but I bet the guy would have pondered his actions and maybe even would have decided not to be such a jerk in the future!)

The last of the five big techniques for building self-discipline is really important: learning to forgive yourself. The Stoics realized that living a Stoic life is a process, not a revelation. People with even the best of intentions inevitably backslide. But the important thing is to keep trying. By continuing to try the Stoics knew we would build more and more self-discipline, and that each time we gained in this area the things that once seemed tough to do would get easier and easier.

Again, science proves this to be true. According to Kelly McGonigal, author of "The Willpower Instinct, How Self-Control Works, Why It Matters, and What You Can Do to Get More of It,"

> Study after study shows that self-criticism is consistently associated with less motivation and worse self-control. It is also one of the single biggest predictors of depression, which drains both "I will" power and "I want" power. In contrast, self-

compassion – being supportive and kind to yourself, especially in the face of stress and failure – is associated with more motivation and better self-control.[xviii]

All of this leads to Nelson Mandela, one of the greatest modern exemplars of Stoicism. Prison wrought a very strong change in him. He began as a man his close friend and law partner Oliver Tambo called "passionate, emotional, sensitive, quickly stung to bitterness and retaliation by insult and patronage."[xix] But he emerged, after 27 years, as one who had become a balanced and measured statesman. This was because in prison "there was little [you] could control. The one thing you could control — that you had to control — was yourself. There was no room for outbursts or self-indulgence or lack of discipline."[xx]

Mandela's biographer points out that prison gave Mandela the opportunity to develop self-discipline. But how did he do it? What were the steps he recalls taking on this journey?

They exactly parallel the Stoic techniques mentioned above.

First, almost so obvious that it escapes recognition right away, prison is an exercise in forced poverty. Everything is taken away. There are no possessions, other than a few curios, maybe a book or two. This absence of material items helps focus the mind on the few simple things that remain. Richard Stengel, author of "Mandela's Way," states that "every evening, [Mandela] painstakingly arranged the few possessions that he was allowed in that tiny cell."[xxi] This lack of possessions stripped away what was inessential to Mandela and helped him focus on disciplining himself, a process that almost seems visible in the way he established a ritual around those few possessions each evening.

Likewise, in terms of self-forgiveness, Mandela's actions and thoughts echo in many places what James Stockdale said of being held prisoner in Vietnam:

"Hardly an American came out of that experience [torture] without responding something like this when first whispered to by a fellow prisoner next door: 'You don't want to talk to me; I am a traitor.' And because we were equally fragile, it seemed to catch on that we all replied something like this: 'Listen, pal, there are no virgins here. You should have heard the kind of statement I made up. Snap out of it. We're all in this together.'"[xxii]

In comparison, for Mandela "prison steeled him but it broke many others. Understanding that made him more empathetic, not less. He never lorded it over those who could not take it. He never blamed anyone for giving in. Surrendering was only human. Over the years, he developed a radar and a deep sympathy for human frailty. In some way, he was fighting for the right of every human being not to be treated the way he had been."[xxiii]

As can be seen here, these experiences in self forgiveness were both a result of and contributor to increased self-discipline.

Mandela also practiced a certain amount of fake positivity while in prison. He was "acutely aware of how he was perceived by his colleagues" in prison and how he must put on a brave face because he "could not let his side down; everyone saw or knew instantly if [he] backed down or compromised."[xxiv] While this focuses on the big picture issues at stake, it is easy to see how the attitude required of Mandela during these times did not allow him to indulge in an outward display of emotion but required, instead, a certain amount of manipulation of how he would be seen: posture, facial expression, tone of voice, choice of words, all these things were the cues upon which his colleagues based their 'acute' awareness.

Mandela's use of negative visualization isn't as pointedly documented as a means of building self discipline, but it is present in one of the most significant changes he brought about in himself and in his life's work. When he went to jail, he was the leader of the militant faction of the ANC. His motto, and one of his most famous lines — which he used to shore up his group's adherence to the ANC's militant position while in prison — was that "Only free men can negotiate; prisoners cannot enter into contracts."xxv However, Mandela eventually changed this position. He decided to negotiate (and was widely criticized by other hardline leaders in the ANC), because he realized that the worst that could happen in a negotiation was not as bad as the worst that could happen, the worst which was beginning to happen, in a civil war between black and white populations in South Africa. Mandela used negative visualization to help himself reflect on his own position, and to change the position of his party. This had almost saintly results.xxvi

Although we all won't be Nelson Mandela, although we all won't be put through the finishing fires of a similar 27-year ordeal in prison, we can use the same techniques to improve our self-discipline and our lives.

In building self-discipline, we must remember that the goal is to establish a *practice* of discipline and that such a practice, like any other skill, requires care, effort, and an allowance for failure and improvement.

Ryan Holiday sums up this process — both reflection and reaction — that leads to self-discipline:

> Subconsciously, we should be constantly asking ourselves this question:
> **Do I need to freak out about this?**
> And the answer — like it is for astronauts, for soldiers, for doctors, and for so many other professionals — must be:
> No, because I **practiced** for this situation and I can control myself. Or, No, because I caught myself and I'm able to **realize** that that doesn't add anything constructive.[xxvii]

In the end, if you do slip up and freak out, that's okay too. Forgive yourself like Stockdale and his fellow POWs. Recognize that this is a journey. Challenge yourself to do better and to focus on what matters, to reflect on relative importance. Whittle things down to their essentials and concentrate on them, so that you create a simple learning environment like Mandela's prison. From that spot you can grow and operate from a place of gratitude. By building the self-confident skill of discipline and by applying your rational mind to understand what is and what isn't in your control, you'll be well on the way to making a big change in your life.

CHAPTER 3
What It Means to Live a Virtuous Life

If you're losing your soul and you know it, then you've still got a soul left to lose. Bukowski

In contrast to most religions and doctrines that provide a roadmap for how to behave, Stoicism offers practical advice for how to live better in the here and now. It prescribes certain ideals of virtue, but it does so within a framework based not on conditions necessary to achieve the rewards of a hypothetical afterlife, but to be rewarded in this life. Stoicism addresses the immediacy and the modernity implied in Bukowski's quote above. We're all losing a bit of our 'soul' in this day and age but, in being alive, in this world, we don't need to look to a next life or an afterlife to do something about it. We control things now. We can lead a good life. Stoicism offers both redemption and reward now, in this life.

Although there are many Stoic virtues – the primary ones are often cited as **wisdom, justice, courage,** and **moderation** – there is another virtue that gets talked about even more. This virtue is both part of the process and part of the reward of living well – **tranquility**.

Let me tell you a little story about tranquility and how I began to find it (the hard way!) in my own life.

A while back I took my girlfriend – now my wife – to the movies. I'd just gotten a new job, straight out of college, and was making good money for the first time in my life. This was when fancy movie theaters were just starting to come into fashion, places that are common enough now with reclining seats, waiters ready to bring three course meals, adult beverages, the whole nine yards. I was going to splurge, spend some of my newfound wealth, and impress my girl.

Only this was back in the beginning years for fancy theaters, the Beta test years.

The show that we went to see was pretty popular, so popular, in fact, that they'd sold out.

I had tickets. But I didn't have reserved seats.

I thought all the seats in a place like that would be reserved. They are now days, probably to prevent situations just like what I experienced, showing up with a very promising date and then — ugh — not being able to sit together in those wonderfully comfortable seats. There were kinks in the process. And I got swept up by this particular one.

Now, like I said, this incident became an important step for me on my personal Stoic journey, an important lesson in tranquility.

You see: I got mad.

Not road-rage mad, but mad enough.

The idea crossed my mind to cause a bit of a scene. Throw a moderate-sized man-tantrum in order to get this situation with the non-reserved seat resolved to my satisfaction.

But I held myself in check. And it was lucky I did because, just a few minutes later, one row in front of that spot where I was on the verge of causing a royal ruckus, I realized the owner of my company and his *wife* were seated. I would have made myself look like a really bad person in front of him if I had started yelling at the waiter or the theater manager. Instead, he turned around, greeted me, introduced his wife, and said, "Glad to have run into you, George."

It became an episode we joked about down the road several times.

And I like to think that my maturity and tranquility in this situation probably impressed my girlfriend too. At least she hasn't held it against me too much!

So, I held my temper. I didn't let the situation disturb my tranquility to the point where I made a bad decision. And I learned that – in matters of virtue – it is important to act like someone is watching you at all times. Because you never know, like in that theater, whether your boss, your future boss, or even your future wife will be judging you and deciding what sort of person you are.

There is a process to inculcating tranquility in your life and your actions.

It's a road, a journey, toward virtue.

And it doesn't happen all at once.

First, you develop an ability to discern what is and isn't in your control, like we discussed in the first chapter.

Then you work on self-discipline to make decisions about the things you can control, the subject of our discussion in the chapter just before this.

After that, or at the same time if you can, you begin to cultivate tranquility in order to have the mental space and the clarity, the presence-of-mind, to think quickly and without a cloud of emotion surrounding every situation.

As sub-steps in cultivating that tranquility, I suggest the following:

1. Work on recognizing when your tranquility gets disrupted

2. Practice behaving as if you're being observed, like having an imaginary person hold you accountable for your actions

3. Soon you will no longer need to pretend you're being watched, the virtue and tranquility will become automatic; you will internalize this state of being

4. Keep tranquility with you everywhere, both because it brings joy and because it continues to facilitate clear-headed decision making

5. Repeat these steps, like a feedback loop, in tougher and tougher situations so that – even if like Nelson Mandela or James Stockdale – you must endure deprivation and danger, you'll maintain your inner tranquility

These steps should be considered unending. You'll grow in them. You'll take tranquility to ever-deeper places in yourself. And you'll see your decision-making improve at every step.

What tranquility promises is the space for decision-making. But it is also a reward of its own. True tranquility allies itself with joy. It frees the mind and the heart to contemplate beauty and life. For these reasons tranquility is not just the object of Stoic endeavor but also a key component on the journey. Epictetus says of this correlation between virtue and tranquility: "If virtue promises good fortune and tranquility and happiness, certainly also the progress towards virtue is progress towards each of these things."xxviii

Every action, thought, or deliberate inaction should work to produce tranquility. And from tranquility, in something of a self-improving feedback loop, we can make better choices because we will be less distracted by emotion or by false (outside of our control) priorities. From a place of tranquility, we will be better able to choose goodness in all things we do. Not just any sort of goodness. Practical goodness. Tranquility is the reward and the **path to redemption** at one and the same time. It is the end state, sure, but the end-state is what moves us and invigorates us, rather than being a prize we win and then say, okay, what's next.

Tranquility is prize and path at one and the same time.

Whoa. Pause for a second and think about that!

Tranquility.

The word isn't too big.

It isn't too complicated.

But, boy, is it loaded with potential misconceptions!

Let's take a moment and think through some of those misconceptions. Say, for instance, if you were to tell your neighbor or your aunt or your best friend that you've begun practicing tranquility, what will they think of?

When you say 'tranquility' to someone it likely conjures up images of a monk at some mountain shrine sitting cross-legged, chanting, detached and unperturbed by the busy happenings of the unenlightened masses below. Or perhaps, in a less religious framework, a person will think of tranquility and imagine sipping an icy beverage in a hammock slung between palm trees on some isolated, pristine beach. Or fishing, just you and a good friend or two in a boat somewhere, nothing but the sound of birds and gently lapping water. In short, tranquility often suggests a withdrawal and separation from the work of living, from the daily grind, the worries, the rat race of our modern lives.

But that is not at all what tranquility means to a Stoic.

Seneca urges us toward virtue and tranquility (also calling us to focus on the here and now, rather than on a future hypothetical 'afterlife') when he says:

> Now while the blood is hot you should make your way with vigour to better things. In this kind of life you will find much that is worth your study: the love and practice of the virtues, forgetfulness of the passions, the knowledge of how to live and die, and a life of deep tranquility.[xxix]

Nowhere does Seneca suggest that virtue be practiced, or tranquility attained, in circumstances of isolation. In fact, judging by his life, or by the life of

Marcus Aurelius or Cato, the best place to work on virtue and tranquility is right in the middle of the messiest parts of life. Seneca did not forego any worldly endeavors: he was not just an advisor to Emperor Nero but also an extremely influential (and wealthy) banker. He was in the midst of the maelstrom of Roman politics, really its master. Yet he practiced a Stoic life, and likely his successes and the sagacity of his advice to Nero were both based on his understanding and application of Stoic principles. The same can be said for Marcus Aurelius, whose private notebooks – now called his **Meditations** – are filled with examples drawn from his daily duties ruling Rome. They often are formatted as earnest exhortations directed at himself to **not give in** to the temptation of withdrawing from the world, but instead to engage more fiercely, more justly, and more tranquilly with the subjects and conditions of his rule and his daily life. And Cato, who stood up to Caesar, never withdrew except when he was forced into exile. He was a walking, talking admonition to other men and women in Rome for how to practice poverty and self-denial (though sometimes, as in his famous divorce of Marcia because **he loved her too much** and felt himself tempted away from self-denial by his adoration of her, he seems not to have given himself enough leeway in terms of self-forgiveness.)[xxx]

The examples these men set in their engagement with the world around them draws the distinction between Stoicism and other religious creeds or doctrines into sharper definition. Where now, in this modern age, people often struggle with the applicability of religion to modern life, often finding religious precepts ineffective for dealing with modern problems and the question of virtue in modern life, Stoicism provides a practical roadmap and gives us examples of very successful Stoic leaders. This roadmap and the examples of these early Stoic leaders show how the practice of virtue and tranquility in the midst of a bustling life can produce good.

Let's look more closely at another, more modern Stoic and his practice of goodness and tranquility: Benjamin Franklin.

In 1726, when he was only 20 years old, Franklin set a very lofty goal for himself. He said:

> I conceiv'd the bold and arduous project of arriving at moral perfection. I wish'd to live without committing any fault at any time; I would conquer all that either natural inclination, custom, or company might lead me into.[xxxi]

To accomplish this goal, Franklin laid out 13 virtues that closely replicate much of the Stoic prescription for living. These goals were: temperance, silence, order, resolution, frugality, industry, sincerity, justice, moderation, cleanliness, tranquility, chastity, and humility. Of tranquility (or *tranquillity* as he spells it!) Franklin provides exactly the same definition as the Stoics.

Compare:

Franklin – "TRANQUILLITY: Be not disturbed at trifles, or at accidents common or unavoidable."[xxxii]

Marcus Aurelius – "Is your cucumber bitter? Throw it away. Are there briars in your path? Turn aside. That is enough. Do not go on and say, 'Why were things of this sort ever brought into this world?' neither intolerable nor everlasting - if thou bearest in mind that it has its limits, and if thou addest nothing to it in imagination. Pain is either an evil to the body (then let the body say what it thinks of it!)-or to the soul. But it is in the power of the soul to maintain its own serenity and tranquility . . ."xxxiii

Although Marcus Aurelius' quote is longer, he and Franklin exhort themselves toward exactly the same conclusion. That is, whether something is common or unavoidable, don't let it get to you. Don't let it disturb your tranquility.

Again, Benjamin Franklin was also a man of the world. We remember him mostly as a patriot and an integral creator of American democracy, but we often forget that he was the original American "self-made man" too — scientist, printer, writer, and longtime ambassador to England and France. He did not use his precept of tranquility as an excuse for disengaging with the world. He brought his virtues with him, Stoic virtues, and put them into practice night and day (though history might quibble with at least one of his professed virtues – he is rumored to never have practiced chastity very well).

Those other Stoic virtues – *wisdom, justice, courage,* and *moderation* – are also defined and practiced by Ben Franklin, always with the goal of tranquility in mind.

'Moderation' and 'justice' he exactly duplicates, saying of them: "Avoid extremes; forbear resenting injuries so much as you think they deserve" and "wrong none by doing injuries, or omitting the benefits that are your duty."[xxxiv]

'Courage' finds its best similitude in Franklin's 'resolution' – "Resolve to perform what you ought; perform without fail what you resolve."[xxxv]

And 'wisdom,' though not exactly duplicated, can be seen in most of Franklin's writings, where he was known for having a country-bumpkin styled wisdom, expressed in his Poor Richard's Almanack.[xxxvi] From his 13 Virtues, those that best capture the Stoic sense of 'wisdom' seem to be 'silence' ("speak not but what may benefit others or yourself; avoid trifling conversation") and 'sincerity' ("use no hurtful deceit; think innocently and justly and, if you speak, speak accordingly").[xxxvii]

That we might achieve these virtues, via iterative improvement in our manner and our way of thought, is entirely possible. It won't come without trial and error. It won't come without effort. But the really clever thing is that the reward for virtue itself grows and, in growing, facilitates ever more growth of virtue. That reward, one we can experience here and now, is tranquility.

In the end, the goal of all this is not to meet a standard of behavior designed for non-mortal life. It is to allow us to succeed and to live better now. William Irvine sums up the Stoic concept of virtue by reaffirming this key distinction, saying: "A virtuous individual is one who performs well the function for which humans were designed. To be virtuous, then, is to live as we were designed to live; it is to live, as Zeno put it, in accordance with nature. The Stoics would add that if we do this, we will have a good life."[xxxviii]

And that, a good life, is the goal.

CHAPTER 4
Fearlessness

I will not fear.
Fear is the mind-killer.
Fear is the little-death that brings total obliteration.

I will face my fear.
I will permit it to pass over me and through me.

And when it has gone past
I will turn the inner eye to see its path.
Where the fear has gone there will be nothing

Only I will remain.
-"Litany Against Fear," from the 1965 novel Dune by Frank Herbert

Although this passage comes from a famous science fiction novel, where the protagonist is trying to steel his nerves for the coming of a fantastical giant Sandworm (among many other out-of-this-world challenges), the principle applies equally well to our everyday types of fear: fear of speaking in public, fear of being perceived a certain way, fear of not fitting in, fear of taking an adventure, fear of striking out on our own in business, fear of failure in general — even fear of death. Every day we face, and use our rational (and often irrational) minds to decide how to deal with, all of these many types of fear.

The Stoics have a prescription for fear. They talk about it a lot, what it is, how to recognize it, how to deal with it or overcome it, and even how to turn it to our advantage. Truly, once we get to that point, once we have learned some tools to put fear in its rightful place — as a useful part of our evolved flight-or-fight response and nothing more — then we can stand like the warrior in Dune and see that, after the fear has gone, only we ourselves remain. This results in a liberating feeling and a vantage point from which we will be able to see more clearly and react more steadily and quickly than those whose minds remain clouded and trapped by emotion.

It results in — wait for it! — *Tranquility*.

That's right! All of the Stoic techniques for dealing with fear aim at the same thing: to produce (or to return a person to) a state of tranquility. Because, like we saw in the previous chapter, tranquility allows us space and ease in which to make better decisions, and because it also is a joy and reward in and of itself, the goal of eliminating fear, or at least of reducing it to manageable proportions, directly impacts both the trajectory toward goodness and the state of that goodness itself. Fear impacts our ability to grow toward ever-deeper levels of inner tranquility and it impacts our ability to enjoy tranquility when and wherever it arrives.

The Stoics teach three primary techniques for facing and diminishing fear: reframing, goal setting, and (once again) the use of negative visualization. To these perhaps a fourth technique that of Dune's simple "standing and enduring" should be added. These techniques are related to one another but can also be looked at separately.

Of the first technique − reframing − Epictetus says:

> Men are disturbed not by the things which happen, but by the opinions about the things: for example, death is nothing terrible . . . when, then, we are impeded or disturbed or grieved, let us never blame others, but ourselves, that is, our opinions.[xxxix]

What Epictetus advocates here is to review the source of the fear. If it is based on our perception, or our projection of an idea about how our actions might be perceived by others, whether we think an action will make us look foolish, whether we have a chance to shine or fail, none of that matters. We cannot control what others think or how they approach us and react to us. We can only control how we think and what we do in response to our thoughts.

Robert Greene, in co-writing the book "The 50th Law" with Curtis "50 Cent" Jackson, summarizes 50 Cent's take on how fear and the opinions of others interact:

> There is another, fearless way of approaching your life. It begins by untying yourself from the opinions of others. This is not as easy as it sounds. You are breaking a lifelong habit of continually referring to other people when measuring your value. You must experiment and feel the sensation of not concerning yourself with what others think or expect of you. You do not advance or retreat with their opinions in mind. You drown out their voices that often translate into doubts inside you. Instead of focusing on the limits you have internalized, you think of the potential you have for new and different behavior.

Your personality can be altered and shaped by your conscious decision to do so. We barely understand the role that willpower plays in our actions. When you raise your opinion of yourself and what you are capable of it has a decided influence on what you do. For instance, you feel more comfortable taking some risk, knowing that you are always able to get back up on your feet if it fails. Taking this risk will then make your energy levels rise—you have to meet the challenge or go under, and you will find untapped reservoirs of creativity within you.[xl]

The fear of what others might think of us is a primary concern that a lot of people have trouble escaping. It contributes greatly to the fear of public speaking, for instance. And it plays into our materialistic culture to no small degree. We always want to look good, to have the newest and best toys, and, in general, to keep up with the Joneses. All of that is because we fear what other people think. Such a fear shouldn't be surprising (though it doesn't hold up to rational inspection). Still, we've all seen it happen. And we've all done it to some degree. But, as 50 Cent and Epictetus both say, we have the power to disregard the opinions of others and, in doing so, we unleash not only fearlessness, but we return to a more tranquil state. That tranquil state is the one where the "reservoirs of creativity" can most easily be tapped.

In addition to overcoming the fear of what other people think, we also have our own opinions to deal with. The example Epictetus provides, alluding to our opinion of death, is a good one that we covered earlier. Death is a rational, inescapable fact. Why fear it? It's not easy to be perfectly rational about such a question, but – in doing so, and in practicing and getting continually closer to a place where all things out of our control can be dismissed as not worth worry – we approach a place where tranquility and its benefits accrue more and more deeply and permanently.

As Gavin de Becker writes in **The Gift of Fear**, "When you worry, ask yourself, 'What am I choosing not to see right now?' What important things are you missing because you chose worry over introspection, alertness or wisdom?"[xli]

From a place of tranquility we see things better. We prioritize better. And this leads to the next Stoic technique: goal setting.

The Stoic concept of goal setting is really just the application of an action plan – a goal or series of goals – to the results of our process of deciding what is and what isn't in our control. In choosing goals that are under our control we diminish the fear involved in many endeavors, because we either decide not to worry if something is completely out of our control (like other peoples' opinions of us), or we break bigger, more complicated issues down into subcategories: parts we can control and parts we can't control. We then disregard the uncontrollable elements and formulate plans to work against only the things we do indeed control. Once the uncontrollable elements are removed, the problem will, almost invariably, seem manageable and **not fearsome**. What's more, by deconstructing a large, fearsome problem into these discreet and rational bits, we reframe our obstacles so that they become steps along the way, an actual plan for success broken down into achievable, controllable parts.

Irvine provides a good illustration of this in "A Guide to the Good Life" when he writes:

It is especially important, I think, for us to internalize our goals if we are in a profession in which "external failure" is commonplace. Think, for example, about an aspiring novelist. She must fight and win two battles: master her craft and deal with rejection of her work. [The fear of failure is reduced when] internalizing goals with respect to novel writing. She should have as her goal not something external over which she has little control, such as getting her novel published, but something internal over which she has considerable control, such as how hard she works on the manuscript or how many times she submits it in a given period of time.[xlii]

There is nothing inherently frightening about working hard on a manuscript. There is nothing inherently scary about submitting a manuscript either (although it might be exciting or even a step into the unknown, but for that – the step into an unknown – we can apply Stoicism's third main technique for dealing with fear: negative visualization, which we'll rehash again in a moment).

By breaking down the problem into controllable and non-controllable parts, we reduce the fear factor.

We control and work against the goals that are internal to us, not those that are external.

The whole situation that creates fear in this context dissolves into three main bits: mastering craft (under our control, given enough hard work and perseverance), and then breaking down the fear of rejection or of the unknown more generally into those things we can't control (editorial opinion: don't worry about it), and those things we can control (hard work, number of times we submit a manuscript). This last part draws an important distinction we'll talk about more later because the hard work we put into something and the perseverance we bring to the application of our hard work over time are key skills. They are so important, in fact, that they get chapter all to themselves.

So, the first two techniques for dealing with fear – reframing and goal-setting – both ask us to use logic in order to discern what is and isn't under our control. The third technique – negative visualization – is most useful for that 'unknown' sort of fright, one where logic can, at times, seem like it is not enough.

Still, there is a way to apply logic to the situation.
Here's how.

As mentioned before, what we do in this situation
of facing the unknown is to negatively visualize and ask
ourselves: *what is the worst that can happen?*

Here, logic can lay out the worst possible scenario
and we can rationally weigh the risks and benefits. This
removes fear. Rationality is the enemy of fear and
friend of a thinking, tranquil person. It's the friend of
the 'better human' Stoicism advocates us each to
become.

As stated earlier, when looked at closely the worst-
case scenario is often not so bad at all. And just by
thinking about it, by mentally rehearsing – or even by
practicing worst-case scenarios, like Tim Ferriss'
practice of a regular interval of poverty – we take the
sting out of the consequences, and we maybe even
bring different sorts of simpler joy and gratitude into
our lives. We turn fear into a positive. We show most
of our fears to be imaginary, illusory, and nothing
more than impediments to success. And some of our
fears turn into opportunities for gratitude and for

building internal strength. That step into the unknown can, all on its own, become something positive – which really takes the sting out of any sort of negative we might have visualized.

Stephen Pressfield, in his "War of Art," explains this when he says: "Fear is good. Like self-doubt, fear is an indicator. Fear tells us what we have to do." He goes on to add that, "The professional tackles the project that will make him stretch. He takes on the assignment that will bear him into uncharted waters, compel him to explore unexplored parts of himself."[xliii]

Writing (and submitting a book to editors) is a step into the unknown for a new author. But how, without taking that step, can she ever hope to become an actual professional? Why not just meet that fear and turn it into a positive?

So negative visualization helps to tamp down our unfounded fears and turn them into rational, manageable steps. And, what's more, we should be looking at those things we fear as opportunities in and of themselves. To take little steps into areas we don't know means we will be able to grow. To take little steps into the unknown, weighing the worst-case scenario, will make those little steps to be more like exploration, fun and a little scary, but not insurmountably frightening.

Seneca offers two very wise aphorisms on how negative visualization can reduce the impact of fear.

First, he asserts that: "[A person] robs present ills of their power who has perceived their coming beforehand."[xliv]

And in another place, he says that misfortune weighs most heavily on those who "expect nothing but good fortune"[xlv]

We can't remove all misfortune from our lives. Some things remain beyond our control: external factors.

But we can do our best to prevent external factors from disturbing our tranquility.

And we can reframe our perspective on problems, set internally-controllable goals, and use negative visualization to reduce the cloud of emotion fear often casts over our ability to make rational decisions with regard to the things we can control. When we start to make good decisions about those parts of problems we can control, the problems become less frightening and tend to evaporate in front of our eyes, all except the external / uncontrollable parts. And those, via sheer rational thought delivered via negative visualization, should not cause worry. We can take purposeful steps toward goals that seem fearsome as well, and in doing so force ourselves to grow. All these things are useful techniques.

Robert Greene and 50 Cent make another important point about confronting fear. Closely related to the "reservoirs of creativity" unleashed by fearlessness is the concept of how fearlessness, and confronting our internally controllable situations, increases another key component of the "better human" – *agility*.

They write:

> We live in a culture that offers you all kinds of crutches – experts to turn to, drugs to cure any psychological unease, mild pleasures to help pass or kill time, jobs to keep you just above water. It is hard to resist. But once you give in, it is like a prison you enter that you cannot ever leave. You

continually look outward for help and this severely limits your options and maneuverability. When the time comes, as it inevitably does, when you must make an important decision, you have nothing inside of yourself to depend on.[xlvi]

We will devote an entire chapter to *agility*. The important thing now is to just acknowledge the link between fearlessness, and our cultivation of fearlessness through reframing, setting goals, and negative visualization, and the ability to be agile.

In fact, the link between fearlessness and agility has a third component, tying 50 Cent's thoughts on creativity and agility together into what is almost a mathematical equation:

Fearlessness + Agility = Creativity

These factors are reciprocal. They compound one upon the other. Be fearless. You increase your agility. Be fearless and agile in a situation, or with regard to a project, and you'll discover (and choose) a creative solution.

And remember, throughout all of this, that everyone confronts fear. Fear of all sorts. Some of the most famous people were nearly incapacitated by fear: Thomas Jefferson, for instance, only gave two speeches during eight years as President, and these were so quietly and humbly spoken that no one could hear them! xlvii Lincoln too. And Ghandi.

And those are just a few famous leaders and one fear, the fear of speaking.

As Teddy Roosevelt, one of the most resilient, fearless leaders of modern times famously said:

> It is not the critic who counts; not the man who points out how the strong man stumbles, or where the doer of deeds could have done better. The credit belongs to the man who is actually in the arena, whose face is marred by dust and sweat and blood; who strived valiantly; who errs, who comes again and again, because there is no effort without error and shortcoming; but who does actually strive to do the deeds; who knows great enthusiasms, the great devotions; who spends himself in a worthy cause; who at the best knows in the end the triumph of high achievement, and who at the worst, if he fails, at least fails while daring greatly. xlviii

To be fearless, we must first sort out what we can and cannot control.

Then we apply rational strategies to break down the things we can control into manageable bits; the things we cannot control, as Seneca says, are not worth our worry and can be put into perspective via negative visualization. As we work on the things we can control we grow our agility, our creativity, and our tranquility.

We are well on our way toward becoming the sort of "better humans" who can stand, observe, and remain in that tranquil place of vision and strength once our fears pass through and only we remain. We control what we fear and, in thinking about it and even embracing it purposefully, we can put it to work to help us live better and reach our potential as humans.

Marcus Aurelius really hits the mark about fear, and how we should perceive it, when he reflects: "It is not death that a man should fear, but he should fear never beginning to live."[xlix]

CHAPTER 5

Finding Opportunity in Setbacks

When I was in 10th grade, I faced one of the first real difficulties of my life.

I was failing chemistry.

I'd always been pretty good in school so this was a shock to me. I just wasn't understanding the material and, as a result, the teacher had begun to think of me as stupid. (Never a good situation to be in with a teacher!)

My parents forced me to get a tutor. He was as old school as old-school gets, an ex-professor, and a hard ass. He'd teach me a particular chemistry topic and then give me non-stop problems and drills. While this was certainly painful, especially at the beginning, after a while I ended up doing much harder and more advanced work in his tutoring sessions than I had been doing in my core chemistry class.

I worked my butt off.

And I also had a secret weapon in this tutor.

Before the end of the semester I was the best student in the class and my chemistry teacher, who could hardly believe the turn-around I made, ended up recommending me for AP classes.

"He now knows the answer to my questions before I can even finish asking the questions," this teacher told my parents.

I ended up taking AP coursework for the next two years and my grades improved enough that I got into a good college.

If I hadn't experienced this huge difficulty with Chemistry class in the first place, I would never have improved. I would never have learned to work as hard as I did under my tutor. And I would likely have coasted by instead of pushing myself and getting into all those tougher classes as a precursor to college.

A situation that began by looking, from my perspective – in 10th grade – as an obstacle, became, instead, an opportunity.

Just as we saw in the previous chapter, the Stoic virtues contribute in no small measure to putting yourself into position to take most obstacles and turn them into stepping stones on your own personal journey toward success, toward becoming a better human and living well now. The agility we have when we are fearless, the fearlessness we can fill our hearts and minds with when we act from a place of tranquility, and the knowledge that we should only worry about things in our control: these are the keys to transforming seemingly immovable obstacles into unexpected advantages.

Ryan Holiday provides an explanation of this and some strategies for how to begin turning obstacles into milestones in his book "The Obstacle is the Way." He says:

> Seen properly, everything that happens—be it an economic crash or a personal tragedy—is a chance to move forward. Even if it is on a bearing we did not anticipate. There are a few things to keep in mind when faced with a seemingly insurmountable obstacle. We must try:
>
> - To be objective
> - To control emotions and keep an even keel
> - To choose to see the good in a situation
> - To steady our nerves
> - To ignore what disturbs or limits others

- To place things in perspective
- To revert to the present moment
- To focus on what can be controlled

> This is how you see the opportunity within the obstacle. It does not happen on its own. It is a process—one that results from self-discipline and logic.[1]

These words could have been taken almost directly from Epictetus, Marcus Aurelius, Seneca, or any of the other early Stoic philosophers. But, wow! How relevant they are for today's world too! They focus on resetting tranquility, achieving an objective viewpoint on the problem, and then focusing on what is actually in our control.

Once we've done these things, once we've identified a problem and reoriented our minds to start looking for opportunity in the problem, there are several well-tested strategies for starting to turn the problem on its head and make it both less fearsome and a step along the way to success. Remember, though, that these things work best once we've separated the internal problems (those we control) from the external problems (those we don't control and shouldn't worry about).

Here are the techniques:

The Flanking Maneuver

Don't tackle the problem head-on. See if there is a different approach. Like a military unit trying to seize an enemy bunker on a hilltop, instead of running right up the hill into the waiting guns, go around the backside and come up where the guns aren't pointed. (This is, of course, an analogy. But useful – if you're not a Marine – to take a look at other, more mundane problems in the same way. Ask yourself: can I approach this differently?) The view from the top of that metaphorical hill, then, will be gorgeous and the objective likely much less difficult to achieve than it would have been if you took the direct route.

Breaking a Big Problem Down

We covered this in some detail in the last chapter, but it is worth repeating here because it really helps in problem solving. The Stoic way to break down a problem into component parts is first to ask yourself, what parts of this do I control? (What is an internal problem and what is an external problem?) Toss all the parts that you don't control into the bin of "not worth worrying about." This will likely contain some potentially catastrophic things, like death. But, on sober and rational reflection, it really isn't worth fretting over things that are out of our control (though this will take some serious effort to re-train your mind: again, think of how hard it is to rationally dismiss things like other peoples' opinions, which we just can't control!) Once we've washed away the external, uncontrollable parts of a problem, we can turn our objective, un-clouded attention to the smaller bits of a problem that remain: how much effort we put into learning something, how much persistence we apply to a problem. The big original problem, when tackled piece by piece with effort and persistence, and with the creativity that comes from not clouding your mind with the emotion of trying to control external factors, will be easier to handle. It will almost seem to dissolve in front of your eyes. In aggregate, once the small parts have been tackled, you'll end up with success – often creatively and from unexpected directions.

Iterate Toward Improvement

This strategy is all the rage now, and for good reason: it works! <u>Borrowing from</u> computer design / coding and engineering, or <u>agile project management</u> processes, the concept is to <u>approach a solution by rapidly iterating through imperfect solutions.</u> It's another way to scale the proverbial hill without walking directly into the machine-gun nest. As one designer, with the perfect name 'Stoic_Arnie', wrote on Reddit regarding his remote-work team's process, "Much of what you see is very iterative. <u>We know where we're trying to go, but the ins-and-outs of how we get there are in constant flux.</u>"[li] This approach works well for any obstacle, not just for computer-related design and engineering. Don't expect perfection on the first try. And keep trying. <u>Make it better gradually and by constantly refining and improving.</u>

Re-imagine the Problem

Sometimes the best strategy for turning a problem into a stepping-stone is just to re-gear your own internal perspective and approach the problem as if it isn't a problem at all (see how I did that: internal = controllable; external = don't fret about it, no matter how terrible the situation. We're going to keep using these words over and over. They're key.) A good example of this is the case of Amy Purdy. Amy lost both her legs due to disease. Of course that is horrible, not a situation anyone wishes to experience, especially if your goal in life is to become a world-renowned snowboarder. Amy took a different perspective on the problem, though. She invented prosthetics to allow her to snowboard and put in the effort to rise to the top of the para-athlete world. She started a company to market her prosthetic innovations. And now, for good reason, she's also a sought-after inspirational speaker with a killer Ted Talk to her credit. She seized the setback, the hardship of losing her legs, and turned it into the opportunity upon which her success has been based.[lii]

The Direct Approach

Sometimes climbing that hill right into the most withering machine gun fire is not only expedient but also the best method too, especially if you've tried some of the other approaches: flanking the problem, re-imagining the problem, breaking the problem down into little, controllable parts, and even iterating through various forms of failure until you reach something that, while not perfect, gets the job done. This Direct Approach borrows a bit from the strategy Amy Purdy used – looking at a problem a different way. The thing, here, is that instead of just looking at your problem a different way, you simply refuse to see the matter as a problem at all. Could Amy Purdy do that with her situation? No. It would be foolish and unrealistic to view her situation as unproblematic. But turning that problem toward good, making it a part of the solution, and using it to elevate herself – all that worked; she re-imagined the problem as a stepping-stone. However, in this direct-attack technique, the secret is to simply refuse to see the problem as a problem at all. Instead, you approach the problem by being so stinking good at what you do that you turn what would be a problem for anyone else into a statement of excellence (this, most likely, means that you've put a ton of hard work and perseverance into your skillset beforehand!)

A good example of this last technique is Michelangelo and his famous Sistine Chapel ceiling. Michael Michalko, writing about famous failures, beautifully explains how Michelangelo triumphed in this situation:

> [Michelangelo's] competitors once tried to set him up for failure or force him to forego a commission because of the possibility of failure. Michelangelo's competitors persuaded [Pope] Junius II to assign to him a relatively obscure and difficult project. It was to fresco the ceiling of a private chapel. The chapel had already been copiously decorated with frescoes by many talented artists. Michelangelo would be commissioned to decorate the tunnel-vaulted ceiling. In this way, his rivals thought they would divert his energies from sculpture, in which they realized he was supreme. This, they argued, would make things hopeless for him, since he had no experience in fresco, he would certainly, they believed, do amateurish work as a painter. Without doubt, they thought, he would be compared

unfavorably with Raphael, and even if the work were a success, being forced to do it would make him angry with the Pope, and thus one way or another they would succeed in their purpose of getting rid of him. Michelangelo, protesting that painting was not his art, still took on the project. In every way it was a challenging task. He had never used color, nor had he painted in fresco. He executed the frescos in great discomfort, having to work with his face looking upwards, which impaired his sight so badly that he could not read or look at drawings save with his head turned backwards, and this lasted for several months. In that awkward curved space, Michelangelo managed to depict the history of the Earth from the Creation to Noah, surrounded by ancestors and prophets of Jesus and finally revealing the liberation of the soul. His enemies had stage-managed the masterpiece that quickly established him as the artist genius of the age.[liii]

Michelangelo didn't iterate toward success. He didn't re-think the problem. He didn't take a flanking route to overcome it. He didn't break the problem down into component parts. Just through the powers of sheer effort and skill – skill, which we'll find out later is a product of ability multiplied by effort, which makes effort twice as valuable over the long run! – he turned what was a set-up for failure into a resounding, ageless triumph.

You too can do that.

Whether the problem is big or small, try these techniques: flanking, re-imagining, breaking the problem down into subparts (controllable and not), and, if all else fails or if you know you're just so darn good you can go for it, then use the Direct Approach.

To decide which of these techniques, or which combination of several of these techniques, you should use, it will be helpful at the beginning, when you're first staring the problem in the face, to take a moment to collect your thoughts. Deepak Chopra suggests the following meditation process for thinking about and overcoming obstacles, which will help you achieve tranquility for fearless decision-making and which will lead you through some of the steps to visualize the problem in a non-threatening and creative way. Chopra suggests, "as you move through each self-reflection question, allow yourself a minute or two for contemplation" and then, at the end, to have a journal handy to write down any solutions or impressions that occur to your tranquil, creative mind. Here are his suggested steps:

- Sit comfortably and close your eyes.
- Begin to take slow deep breaths, in and out through your nose.
- Allow your shoulders to relax and your torso to soften with every exhale.
- Bring into your awareness an area of your life where an obstacle is present.
- Think about when, where, and how this obstacle began.
- Ask yourself who or what triggers the problem. What thoughts and emotions are prevalent when the obstacle is present?
- Now bring your attention to the cost of this obstacle. How does it affect your ability to be, do and have the things you want in life? How does it affect those around you? Note: negative visualization might be useful here too!
- Next, see what can be available to you if you overcome this obstacle and are able to move powerfully forward in your life. Note: Positive visualization!
- Consider anyone you know who has already overcome this kind of obstacle. Who was it? What approach did they take?
- Now think about how you might do things differently than the way you have been up to this

point, perhaps including some approaches others have taken.

Note: this is like the flanking approach to that hill!

- Next, invite in an intention for a creative solution to come forth. Ask your Self or the Universe for guidance in how best to navigate and overcome this obstacle.
- And now, imagine your life as if the obstacle was dissolved and you are now standing in the life you have created by design.
- After you have a positive internal representation (an image, sound, or feeling) of being free from this obstacle, spend a few moments in quiet contemplation before slowly coming out of your meditation.[liv]

What you will likely find, after thinking about your obstacle in this meditative way, and after applying some other Stoic techniques to approaching the problem, is that the problem no longer seems so daunting. Creativity might inspire you to approach the problem as an opportunity, maybe even as fun. Tranquility will give you the fearlessness to make a decision and move forward. You will likely find, like I did with my 10th Grade Chemistry tutoring or like Amy Purdy did in overcoming her physical limitations, that an application of effort and a new viewpoint on the problem will open doors to realms of success you hadn't imagined before.

> In this way, what seems like a dour and un-fun methodology, this Stoic mindset toward problems, actually produces success AND joy. As William Irvine writes, "One might imagine that the Stoics, because they go around contemplating worst-case scenarios, would tend toward pessimism. What we find, though, is that the regular practice of negative visualization has the effect of transforming Stoics into full-blown optimists."[lv]

We can add to this use of negative visualization the techniques discussed above: flanking our problems, breaking them down into parts, re-imagining them, iterating through them toward goodness, and just attacking them head-on. All those methods tend to produce fearless optimism in those of us who live the Stoic lifestyle. And, even as you work hard and apply perseverance to your problems – the two keys to success that we'll discuss next – you'll find that joy and tranquility spring unbidden from these endeavors. For what is better in life than to meet our problems with an arsenal of methods that allows us to turn obstacles into the very platforms (or like Michelangelo, the very ceilings!) of our ever-evolving, lifelong masterpiece of living well?

CHAPTER 6
Hard Work & Perseverance

If you always put limits on everything you do, physical or anything else, it will spread into your work and into your life. There are no limits. There are only plateaus, and you must not stay there, you must go beyond them. - Bruce Lee

In the previous chapter we examined strategies for turning the mountains we face, the swamps, rivers, forests, and canyons that are our obstacles in life, into the very means by which we achieve success. Common to all those obstacles, but also necessary for navigating the plateaus – which can seem sometimes to stretch into infinity! – are two characteristics we can teach ourselves.

These are hard work and perseverance.

The two concepts are different from each other but also correlated. When merged together, they might be expressed by a single term: ***effort***.

That term is useful in its own right. And we'll pay some serious attention to it at the end of this chapter.

But now, to start, it will be useful to highlight the differences between hard work and perseverance. In order to make them effective, you must understand and be able to apply them both. They are easy concepts to understand, but tougher to put into action.

The simpler of the two, as far as implementation, is hard work. It really means 'how much effort – whether mental, physical, or emotional – you put into a particular task.' And, importantly, hard work as we will define it tends to be limited in time. It is the application of effort, or work, in a robust and vigorous way, for the limited duration of a task.

Almost everyone can do this. Almost everyone has done it. I bet you can think of a hundred or a thousand examples of hard work you've done to achieve certain tasks, right? Burning the midnight oil to study for a test. Building something. Running a marathon. Organizing an event.

All of these things take a certain amount of hard work.

Perseverance, on the other hand, is tougher to implement. But what it does is allow you to extend the effects of hard work over time and achieve mastery of a problem. For example, you might be able to just go out and run a marathon simply by exerting yourself to the max (hard work). But to really run a marathon well – to prevent injury or to achieve a personal record time (something internally 'controllable' – whereas a goal like 'winning a marathon' isn't internally controllable) requires a lot of training. The application of hard work over time to achieve the goal of training for that personal record is what we will call perseverance. Same for other problems: the application of hard work to organizing a single event will likely allow you to pull the event off. Where perseverance comes in is when you apply hard work over a long duration with the goal of throwing the best possible event. This will likely involve some level of training. But it will also help you achieve larger goals too (if you so desire), perhaps positioning you as the best event planner around and allowing you to start a successful business.

Perseverance also implies a capacity to let yourself fail and then get back up again and attack the problem from another angle – the iterative process we described before. Maybe flanking it the next time, or breaking the problem down into parts, or reimagining it. Improving not only the process but also your ability, in general, to overcome obstacles and turn them into platforms for success.

Jacob August Riis, the late-1800s muckraker journalist known for working with and photographing the poor of New York City, describes what perseverance is when he writes: "When nothing seems to help, I go and look at a stonecutter hammering away at his rock, perhaps a hundred times without as much as a crack showing in it. Yet at the hundred and first blow it will split in two, and I know it was not that last blow that did it, but all that had gone before."[lvi]

Hard work is the effort of the single hammer blow. It takes strength and talent developed over time to bring the hammer into contact on the rock in the right way, at the right angle. But the rock doesn't break with just one blow.

Perseverance, then, is the ability to look at the unbroken rock and to have the confidence, stamina, and patience to continue blow after blow. It is also the ability, when the hammer doesn't quite do the trick, to step back from the problem, not quitting but reassessing. Perhaps applying a flanking maneuver, perhaps working at the stone chip by chip, with glancing blows, rather than trying to cut through the middle. Perseverance is failing and then not giving up but hammering again in a different way.

Thomas Edison exemplifies perseverance. As Ryan Holiday explains, "In 1878, Thomas Edison wasn't the only person experimenting with incandescent lights. But he was the only man willing to test six thousand different filaments — including one made from the beard hair of one of his men — inching closer each time to the one that would finally work."[lvii]

The analogy of the stonecutter, and also the image of a plateau, bring up an important point about hard work and perseverance. Often, when beginning a task, it can be tough to motivate ourselves. It can be tough to see the end toward which we are working. So, here, that important Stoic principle of dividing up a problem into those things we can control and those we cannot comes in handy, whether it is a short term problem like cracking open a stone, or a longer term problem like becoming the best stone cutter possible. When we focus on the things we can control, we can set goals for ourselves that are both realistic and motivating because they are within our power to achieve. We eliminate frustration and bitterness at what we might, otherwise, perceive to be menial, undistinguished, and massively repetitive tasks that we must do in order to build expertise and persevere until the larger goals are within our reach.

There's an awesome story about John F. Kennedy visiting NASA that speaks to this process of using longer-term, controllable goal-setting to help us persevere through menial tasks. During a tour of the space center in 1962, Kennedy noticed a janitor carrying a broom. He walked over to the man (like a good politician will) and introduced himself. Then he asked the janitor: "What are you doing?"

The janitor said, "Well, Mr. President, I'm helping put a man on the moon."

The janitor probably didn't have an ambition to clean floors, to sweep up after people. But by linking his work — which was no doubt repetitive and required perseverance for him to do well day after day — to the larger goal of the organization, he attacked the controllable part of his work task and thereby helped the organization become proficient. His focus on a controllable goal helped him develop perseverance and impress the President. Perhaps, by his example, he provided inspiration and helped Kennedy persevere too!

Robert Greene and 50 Cent contribute a similar perspective on the menial, hard labor necessary to master important skills. They start by talking about the million distracting amusements we tend to occupy ourselves with when we should be applying hard work and perseverance to become better humans. Then they go on to write:

> These [distracting] entertainments have a faster pace than the time we spend at work. Work then is experienced as something boring—slow and repetitive. Anything challenging, requiring effort, is viewed the same way—it's not fun; it's not fast. If we go far enough in this direction, we find it increasingly difficult to muster the patience to endure the hard work that is required for mastering

any kind of craft. It becomes harder to spend time
alone. Life becomes divided between what is
necessary (time at work) and what is pleasurable
(distractions and entertainment).[lviii]

Beyond the menial, repetitive nature of the tasks
we're required to do in order to achieve excellence in a
field, there is another reason people often decide not to
apply hard work and perseverance to a problem: *the
excuse of talent.*

Talent is usually thought of as a good thing.

But, very often, it − or the perception that we lack it
− becomes another handy excuse for us to stop trying.
For us to stop persevering.

"I just don't have talent" is a thought that people
use who don't want to put in the hard work, or − even
if they don't mind the hard work − aren't approaching
the issue with a necessary dollop of Stoic fearlessness.
The opinions of others and the fear of failure both
conspire to make such people think they shouldn't put
in the effort (hard work and perseverance) required to
develop what talent they *do have*, and so the excuse of
'not being talented' at something comes in handy.

Friedrich Nietzsche condemns this very same excuse of 'lacking talent' when he writes: "Our vanity, our self-love, promotes the cult of genius. For if we think of genius as something magical, we are not obliged to compare ourselves and find ourselves lacking . . . To call someone 'divine' means: 'here there is no need to compete."[lix]

Again, Robert Greene and 50 Cent provide useful commentary: "All human activities involve a process of mastery. You must learn the various steps and procedures involved, proceeding to higher and higher levels of proficiency. This requires discipline and tenacity—the ability to withstand repetitive activity, slowness, and the anxiety that comes with such a challenge."[lx] And then they add, as a reflection on keeping the larger goal at the front of your mind in order to withstand and eventually grow into enjoying the very process of perseverance: "First, having the larger goal will lift your mind out of the moment and help you endure the hard work and drudgery. Second, as you become better at this task or craft, it becomes increasingly pleasurable."[lxi]

We already looked at Thomas Edison and the secret to his 'genius' (which some people have dismissed as a 'talent' for organization and experimentation, but which was, instead, mostly an amazing fearlessness and tenacity). How about another genius?

Sir Isaac Newton.

He invented calculus, quantified gravity as a force, and his theories on how the world works were so influential that they – known as Newtonian Physics – weren't seriously challenged until Einstein.

That's some serious talent, right?

Wrong.

His biography states: "After receiving his bachelor's degree in 1665, Newton stayed on for his master's, but an outbreak of the plague (a highly infectious and deadly disease often carried by rats) caused the university to close. Newton returned to [his parents' estate at] Woolsthorpe for eighteen months, from 1666 to 1667, during which time he performed the basic experiments and did the thinking for his later work on gravitation (the attraction the mass of the Earth has for bodies near its surface) and optics (the study of light and the changes it experiences and produces). [During this time] Newton also developed his own system of calculus (a form of mathematics used to solve problems in physics)."[lxii]

While the outbreak of plague and the inability to continue studying for his masters' degree might, at first, have seemed like an obstacle, Newton used that solitary time to achieve some seriously notable things. It wasn't mere 'talent.' The ideas for these things, though gravity might, indeed, have been inspired by a falling apple somewhere on the grounds of his parents' bucolic estate, didn't spring into his mind unbidden. These were, as Robert Greene and 50 Cent point out, developed within the "period of forced isolation and repetitive labor" that the 18 months of plague caused, a period when his classmates and peers were "paralyzed by fear and boredom."[lxiii] But rather than say, 'this is an obstacle to my education' or – worse – 'I don't have the talent to work on these problems myself' Isaac Newton applied hard work and perseverance over a fairly long time to achieve amazing results and change science and math forever.

Perhaps most importantly in the discussion of how key hard work and perseverance are to achievement is the formula developed by Angela Duckworth in her research on **grit**. Hers is not a tough equation but it's powerful, and perhaps life-changing once you realize the implications and start to implement them in your life.

What Duckworth found is that effort (remember, we're saying effort is hard work + perseverance) counts twice as much as talent in the process of achieving a goal.

The equation works like this:

$$\textit{Talent x Effort = Skill}^{\text{lxiv}}$$

(So, yes, you have to have some talent to start . . . For instance, although you can let a monkey sit at a typewriter for eternity, the process of him randomly writing a Shakespeare sonnet won't ever be the same as having talent. We need a bit of talent to begin with, but even if − like Amy Purdy − we lose some of the capacity necessary to perform a basic function along the road to our desired achievement, we can, by effort and creativity, still develop skill and reach a point where we can claim success.)

Once we've developed skill, the second half of the equation, is:

Skill x Effort = Achievement[lxv]

Take the baseline modicum of talent (again, that doesn't need to be a LOT of talent, just enough) and apply a whole bunch of effort to it. You produce skill. For Newton these skills were mathematics, physics, a fluidity with equations, and an understanding of where science had so far taken human understanding of natural phenomena.

But then, to reach achievement, we must multiply that skill by effort again. We can have all the skill in the world. But if we don't continue to apply hard work and perseverance over time to our usage of that skill, we end up a disappointment, like a racehorse without fire, or a football player drafted in the first round because of his measurable speed, strength, and size but lacking the heart and the grit to compete. Newton's achievements were in applying mathematics, in understanding mathematics to such a degree that he knew he needed to invent more advanced formulas, and to use those formulas and methodologies to achieve a more precise and insightful description of the natural world.

One more look at this.

There are, you'll notice, only two ingredients for achievement: talent and effort. Skill is a product along the way. And effort counts twice as much. So, while you could legitimately claim you just don't have talent (which I'll probably do whenever someone asks me to dance – I've tried and tried again and I just know now, after much perseverance, that I've genuinely got two left feet) you should really ask yourself if, by applying effort, by applying twice as much effort, you won't be able to build skill and then use that skill to achieve your goals.

Duckworth sums this up, saying: "Without effort, your talent is nothing more than your unmet potential. Without effort, your skill is nothing more than what you could have done but didn't. With effort, talent becomes skill and, at the very same time, effort makes skill productive."[lxvi]

Although we have a whole chapter upcoming on the topic of mentorship, it's important to note how, in this process of perseverance and effort and learning, the presence of a good mentorship climate also makes a difference. In Newton's case, he tended toward functioning as an autodidact, teaching himself once he'd achieved a certain level of proficiency during his undergraduate studies at Cambridge. That, rather than his achievements, resonates more with the term 'genius.' However, for most of us, in her study of grit, Duckworth has found that the network of mentorship helps us develop qualities of perseverance and learn not to think of talent as a genetic quality but as a learned and developed attribute. She writes: "There's a larger ecosystem of adults that extends beyond the nuclear family. All of us are "parents" to young people other than our own children in the sense that, collectively, we are responsible for "bringing forth" the next generation. In this role of supportive but demanding mentors to other people's children, we can have a huge impact."[lxvii]

She goes on to provide the following example, citing comments from two participants in her field studies, Sylvia and Rhonda:

> People assume you have to have some special talent to do mathematics," Sylvia has said. "They think you're either born with it, or you're not. But Rhonda and I keep saying, 'You actually **develop** the ability to do mathematics. **Don't give up!**'
>
> "There have been so many times in my career when I wanted to pack it in, when I wanted to give up and do something easier," Rhonda told me. "But there was always someone who, in one way or another, told me to keep going. I think everyone needs somebody like that.[lxviii]

What have we learned of effort − hard work and perseverance?

First, it is twice as important as talent in our pursuit of achievement.

Second, it helps us both confront the obstacles and endure the plateaus of our problem solving.

Third, it is a learned trait, to be honed by mentorship.

And, fourth, though not yet discussed, but the subject of our next chapter, it requires a certain amount of self-discipline in the process of decision-making in order to keep it focused and moving forward productively. Without self-discipline and good decision-making, effort will be wasted on a million trivial, unfocused activities.

But more on that in a moment.

Let's finish now with a return to the roots of Stoic philosophy.

Always looking on the bright side of negative visualization, Seneca wrote, in his "To Helvia," a good post-script for the idea of perseverance. He said: "Everlasting misfortune does have one blessing, that it ends up by toughening those whom it constantly afflicts."[lxix]

We need not look at perseverance and hard work always in such glum terms, though. It is a way to help us through the worst. But it is also a key tool to bring to bear in the positive situations as well: the 6,000 filaments of Edison or the 18-months of Newton's isolated study and invention. By working hard at a task and by extending passion and effort over time, through failure if need be in an iterative process toward improvement, we will develop skills and press forward toward the achievement of goals and dreams.

PART II: Mind

CHAPTER 7
Decision Making

In the first section of this book we discussed some of the basic principles of Stoicism and how you can use them as a roadmap for self-improvement. This is because Stoic principles aren't composed of esoteric theory. Instead, they're underpinned with really solid (and well-tested) practical philosophy. In fact, that was the whole point of Stoicism, to get away from ideas that had become ever more convoluted and divorced from everyday life, beautiful ideas for sure, like Plato's "ideal forms," but ones that didn't really do all that much to help us live better lives in the here and now. That's what the Stoics were after: how to be a good person and how to use your time on earth to its fullest; how to fulfill your potential. The basic steps of Stoicism that we've covered line up smoothly and progress one after the other, leading you on a logical path toward self-improvement. First, learn to separate what you can control from what you can't. Work on building self-discipline. Understand what a virtuous life is (especially nowadays, when 'virtue' has meanings that are either focused on an afterlife or derived from benign hedonism). Hone a rational fearlessness in your actions. Start looking at setbacks as opportunities. And, last, practice hard work and perseverance.

We've covered each of these principles in a chapter. And we've talked a lot about how they are interlinked. For example, in order to turn setbacks into opportunities you need to be fearless in how you approach that setback, you need to determine whether the obstacle is in your control (or at least partially in your control) so as to make sure you are directing your efforts and your fearlessness at something that will produce results, rather than just frustration, and you likely will need to apply both hard work and perseverance.

The next few chapters are going to refine these principles. They will focus on cutting away extraneity and developing the methods, skills, and mindset that lead to a fulfilling Stoic life, a life well lived. The topics of these chapters will be: Stoic decision-making (which was already touched on a little in our very first chapter about discerning what you can and cannot control!); the importance of mentorship (which was briefly mentioned in the last chapter, with regard to how a good mentor or community-parent network can help teach hard work and perseverance); realism (which ties in with fearlessness and also with knowing what is and isn't in your control); and agility (which was covered in some detail during the chapter on turning setbacks into opportunities: think of the flanking maneuver again). Then in the third part of the book we'll get into the Soul of the matter: being authentic, using the past as a teacher, ensuring we remain and embrace the social nature of our beings, and – very last – a nod to gratefulness.

So, although all these topics have been alluded to or even explained a little over the course of the first part of this book, think of these next chapters as your finishing fire, or your opportunity to polish the rough-cut jewel you may have just discovered in yourself. You've had the basics. Now we're going to go a little deeper into the elements that will take you from a few rewarding first steps to a more vigorous and joy-creating fulfillment of the Stoic lifestyle.

* * * * *

To begin with, when we talk about decision-making, the analogy of the artist or master craftsman again comes to the fore. This time, instead of hammering away at the same stone that Jacob Riis described, our old friend Epictetus provides the imagery. He says, "Just as wood is the medium of the carpenter and bronze is the medium of the sculptor, your life is the medium on which you practice the art of living."[lxx] Practicing the art of living well requires constant decision-making. As we've seen, the best place – the best state of mind – from which to make good decisions is one of tranquility. And tranquility is also both the object and the reward of a Stoic life.

So it's like a triple bonus: object, reward, and facilitator of better decision-making, all rolled up in one.

Once you're in that tranquil state, we've discussed how it is easier to be fearless and also easier to be agile, especially if you've already cleared away the emotions associated with frustration from trying to solve problems that aren't actually in your control (like someone else's opinion of you). Of this, Marcus Aurelius says, "You have power over your mind – not outside events. Realize this, and you will find strength." [lxxi] This is a rational realization and a rational decision, to exert control over one's own mind and perceptions.

It's a good start. But now, let's take decision-making a bit further and add another element of rationality to it.

Here, we suggest that your decisions must not only be made fearlessly and focus on things you can control. They must also start to align with a larger goal structure.

The technique for achieving alignment of your goals derives much from hard work and perseverance, but the overall effect is similar to the equation for velocity: velocity = speed x direction. Note these two components and think about them practically. Speed, without being strongly tied to a physical (or in our case a moral and decision-making direction) is just wasted effort. You could be moving fast but only, really, running in place. You could be a water-molecule agitated to the point of boiling, but if not harnessed to turn the cogs of a generator, all that wild energy goes to waste. It disperses into the air. Nothing actually happens in terms of creating benefits for you or for your goals.

The trick, you see, is to **align your decisions around a goal or goals**. This turns your effort, which might otherwise be unharnessed and wasted, into velocity. It turns your effort into a directed force that will help you achieve.

Angela Duckworth explains the arrow of this motivational compass:

> What I mean by passion is not just that you have something you care about. What I mean is that you care about that **same** ultimate goal in an abiding, loyal, steady way. You are not capricious. Each day, you wake up thinking of the questions you fell asleep thinking about. You are, in a sense, pointing in the same direction, ever eager to take even the smallest step forward than to take a step to the side, toward some other destination.[lxxii]

Aligning our efforts, via making decisions that are based on a steady, long-term passion, rather than spur-of-the-moment whims or capricious desires, helps us persevere. Not only do we stand fast in the face of obstacles, but we do so with a goal at the forefront of our minds so that obstacles don't divert us.

Had our stonecutter hacked away at his stone without a goal in mind, he might have produced nothing more glorious than two smaller stones. But if he was better than that, if he was aligning all the chips and all the polishing toward a single vision – and if he had trained his talents into skill through repetition and effort, he might be Michelangelo, and all that work would be going toward a single passion or toward *La Pieta*: a masterpiece. That is the real secret that turns effort into achievement. It's exactly how Michelangelo got there: talent made doubly strong by two applications of effort. Effort aligned to a vision, to a goal; effort that turns talent into skill and then, applied again, turns skill into achievement. Even when forced into an uncomfortable situation, like painting frescoes, the realignment of Michelangelo's talent and his effort around a new but singular vision and purpose resulted in achievement. Maybe the result of similar effort will not be the Sistine Chapel for you or me. But the principle holds.

Set and follow a decision-making compass. Use your rationality to discard things you can't control. Focus on those things you can control. And focus even more precisely on the things you can control that also align with and bring you closer to your goal(s).

Fearlessness and tranquility allow you to apply your rational powers because they move you past paralyzing guilt and keep you from straying from your goals. So once you've set the conditions to bring that rational mind to bear, you're bringing the full power of thousands, even hundreds of thousands of years of evolution to bear.

The rational mind is what separates humans from animals. The rational mind allows us to make decisions that might be, or seem to be, bad over the short term but end up being good over the long term.

The classic example of this is provided by Robert Pirsig in his book "Zen and the Art of Motorcycle Maintenance." He describes a trap for monkeys that uses the inability of the monkey to rationalize short-term benefits against long-term gain. Oliver Burkeman summarizes Pirsig's anecdote in an article in The Guardian,

> The trap "consists of a hollowed-out coconut, chained to a stake. The coconut has some rice inside which can be grabbed through a small hole". The monkey's hand fits through the hole, but his clenched fist can't fit back out. "The monkey is suddenly trapped." But not by anything physical. He's trapped by an idea, unable to see that a principle that served him well – "when you see rice, hold on tight!" – has become lethal.[lxxiii]

What would we do in this instance, as rational humans? Of course we'd let the rice go. We'd not allow our balled-up fist to keep us in the trap. But the situations we face aren't always as simple as this physical trap. That's why Stoicism argues for the pause, for the creative application of rationality, for us to take a moment, let the clouds of emotion dissipate, and make decisions that might not be in our best interest short term. If our long-term goal is to lose a few pounds and get back to where we were ten years ago, for instance, then we must align our efforts over the short-term, even if they aren't hedonistically joyful right at any particular moment of decision (jogging a few extra miles each week, eating that salad instead of the slab of greasy-delicious DiGiorno). That is rationality in action on a human level, rising above mere animal needs and impulses.

Here, again, the distinction between 'good' and 'bad' decisions must be made rationally. This should never be a subjective call. You should not say, I'm going to eat pizza because it tastes good. And salad because it tastes bad. Those are subjective distinctions, not related to your goal. The concept of 'good,' in this context, should be judged, weighed and judged, only according to how well it aligns your effort(s) with your goal(s). And here, goals very well might be plural. Because you and I usually don't operate with just one goal. We have competing goals in several areas of our lives that tend to overlap. We will need to use rationality again to resolve tension between these goals.

Let me explain.

Sticking with pizza and salad. You might have two goals that conflict in this area. The first, which we've already discussed in some detail, is to lose those ten or twelve pounds. But another goal, maybe even – or likely even – overriding that first goal, could be to spend quality time with a son or daughter. And that son or daughter really wants to go to Chuck-E Cheese. Here you have goal alignments pointing in different directions: do you go to Chuck-E Cheese and not eat pizza? Sure. That's an option (and it's probably the one that pure rationality would list as most certain to meet both your objectives). But there could be a third, deeper goal here, in wanting to bond with your child. Eating together is a good bonding mechanism. Doing so in a place a child enjoys, one with blinking lights and funny creatures that the child will find wonderful and stimulating, can be even more rewarding. So perhaps in this case the desire to align the arrow of your bonding effort trumps your goal of consuming fewer calories. Perhaps, we use our mind to order and sort our priorities, to stack them one against the other. And perhaps, employing that little tranquil pause, where we can really make strides, in a situation like this, is to use our agility, our creativity, and our Stoic strategies to see if there is an alternative solution that satisfies multiple needs: is there a children's play place that offers healthy food too? (Where maybe, also, yet another goal – this one to teach your child to eat well – can get a little effort applied to it!)

This example is just one of many choices we make daily, even hourly, between competing priorities, competing alignments. We make choices big and small, with the point being that little efforts can go a long way, when directed correctly, to build toward bigger goals.

Sorting this all out seems like it would take a massive computer.

Fortunately, we've been blessed with the most massive computer in existence. Right here between our ears.

Although digital computers seem pretty amazing and have become more and more ubiquitous in smart phones and smart appliances and smart houses and even AI, our brains still have the advantage and probably will for a long while.

As a recent article in Quora says:

> Humans are spectacular at several things, including pattern recognition, language abilities, and creative thinking. Computers are rapidly improving at pattern recognition, but most programs still don't do as well as children. A classic example of pattern recognition is face recognition. We are capable of recognizing faces in a variety of contexts. We can even recognize faces that have aged, or are disguised, or are obscured by facial hair. Computers are not nearly as good as humans at such tasks. Humans are more powerful than computers at tasks that are not easily broken into simple steps. The fields of computer science, artificial intelligence, and machine learning are aimed at breaking down problems into 'byte-sized' chunks that are 'digestible' by computers. So for now computers are informational babies — they cannot 'cook' for themselves.[lxxiv]

In fact, other recent research suggests that the computing power of human brains is even greater than realized before. Up until now the computing power of the human brain was calculated mainly by totaling up the activity of a certain part of each nerve cell in the brain, called an axon. Axons can be seen to light up when we are stimulated. But each nerve cell has several dozen smaller structures, called dendrites, which light up as well. Dendrites were originally thought to be nothing more than wiring but now, according to Spencer Smith, a neuroscientist at the University of North Carolina, Chapel Hill, "the bursts of spikes we saw [from dendrites] were hard to believe." Instead of being "isolated, solemn obelisks, by comparison, the dendritic spikes we saw were raucous, dynamic events, with bursts and plateaus. Suddenly, it's as if the processing power of the brain is much greater than we had originally thought."[lxxv]

We're fortunate to have this computing power.

It separates us from animals. It helps us sort through the complex web of priorities for where we place (and, hopefully, align) our efforts. It allows us to use specific techniques, like negative visualization, to overcome fear, anxiety, and false assumptions about what we control and what we do not control so that we can pause in a place of tranquility and make a decision that allows us to free our hand from the trap of immediate gratification.

This is the essence of how to make decisions that lead you ever farther down the road of a Stoic life, toward not only happiness and joy, but fulfillment in the here-and-now. Not every belief system offers that potential. As Robert Greene says in The 50th Law:

> Understand: as an individual you cannot stop the tide of fantasy and escapism sweeping a culture. But you can stand as an individual bulwark to this trend and create power for yourself. You were born with the greatest weapon in all of nature – the rational, conscious mind. It has the power to expand your vision far and wide, giving you the unique capacity to distinguish patterns in events, learn from the past, glimpse into the future, see through appearances.[lxxvi]

CHAPTER 8
Mentorship

If I am walking with two other men, each of them will serve as my teacher. I will pick out the good points of the one and imitate them, and the bad points of the other and correct them in myself. Confucius

We've already discussed mentorship a little, in terms of how it impacts the development of perseverance. But how do you go about finding a mentor? And what do you do with one once you have, finally, identified this illustrious personage?

I'll tackle the first question by providing another little anecdote from my own life, where the main point is this: sometimes you don't get to choose your mentor; sometimes you're not even aware that you're looking for one. The mentor chooses you. Or – poof – there they are in your life and the question really becomes something more like: **Are you ready to receive?**

Here's my situation.

I had a boss years ago with whom I did not often agree. I didn't like the way he managed things. I took umbrage with many of the decisions he made for the team. I held a lot of resentment toward him but I managed to control it, to keep it to a low simmer. And it's a good thing I did.

You see, as my career progressed I grew into a similar role. And I started to see things differently. I started to look at this former boss's decisions differently. I hated those decisions when I was at a lower rung on the ladder but from my new vantage point his decisions started to make more sense. I found myself patterning my own decisions on what I'd observed from him. I was able to take the things he did and then temper them with my personal recollection of how those things sucked for me, in the moment, when I was the underling. I made some adjustments to lessen the effects of those bad points. And I think I was able, by doing this, to walk the line between both of Confucius' mentors: learning by emulation on the one hand while, on the other, learning by avoidance.

Without the experience of both hating that situation and observing that situation I would never have been prepared to take on similar responsibilities and make similar decisions, and doing so in what I hope was a bit better of a way. This unexpected 'mentorship,' even though I never formally said – *hey, I'm going to use this guy as a mentor* – prepared me to succeed.

This is one of the Stoic principles for mentorship. A mentor should not just be someone to look up to but someone to use as a measuring stick for our own actions, both positive and negative.

While the example I gave from my own life touched on both the positive and the negative, Seneca describes the more traditional 'positive mentor' in really excellent detail:

> Choose someone whose way of life as well as words, and whose very face as mirroring the character that lies behind it, have won your approval. Be always pointing him out to yourself either as your guardian or as your model. This is a need, in my view, for someone as a standard against which our characters can measure themselves. Without a ruler to do it against you won't make the crooked straight.[lxxvii]

Seneca's positive mentor comes through loud and clear here. He urges us to pick out someone to pattern ourselves on. In doing so we hope to absorb and emulate the good traits we see.

In the case of the bad example, where you can learn what **not to do**, you can also pick up a couple of additional Stoic benefits (while honing your skills of perseverance!)

The first of these additional benefits is to use the experience to teach yourself not to take things too personally. You build an emotional or mental wall and separate work from the higher goals in your life. Or you find ways to overcome the obstacle the boss presents in order to create success in its place. Both of those exercises will yield insight and tools that come in useful later in your career and life.

The second benefit, especially in the case where the 'bad boss' is a micro-manager or a perfectionist or really hot-tempered – you learn quickly the value of putting your best efforts into a project. You double- and triple-check your work. You micro-manage yourself to the point where the boss can find no flaws. Driving yourself to that level, while it might not be ideal in terms of agility, creativity, or work-life balance, teaches a lesson that can be useful later: an appreciation of your own capacity for excellence.[lxxviii]

A third point to consider with regard to mentors in the office environment, bad or good, is that you must be very careful in trusting their motives. As David D'Alessandro says in Executive Warfare: "Unless your boss is very, very strong, he is likely to have moments of paranoia as you gain power and he suddenly feels your hot breath at the back of his neck . . . So beware the mentor."[lxxix] This might be an over-exaggeration. Beneficent bosses aren't unknown in the workplace. And they often are motivated not only by sheer goodwill, but also by ideas of legacy, and of the more immediate, pressing need to build their teams through actualizing and encouraging their subordinates. Still, it is a point to consider: will you, in lighting your star and setting the world (or at least the lunch-room) ablaze, present a direct threat to your erstwhile mentor? If so, you should examine your approach. That mentor relationship might be more important in the long run than temporary advancement. In fact, it might be important enough (and your rise in the workplace rapid and unavoidable enough, if the mentoring and your other Stoic life-skills are all coming together to help you turn obstacles into successes) that the best course turns out to be parlaying your newfound skills into a job elsewhere: keep the mentor, keep the relationships positive with that particular employer, and go forth to do great things at a safer distance!

This suggests another important topic for consideration in your approach to mentorship: the phases you'll go through in your process of mastery.

First, when you're young, the imperative is to explore. A mentor should facilitate this exploration. As Angela Duckworth says in Grit,

> Encouragement during the early years is crucial because beginners are still figuring out whether they want to commit or cut bait. Accordingly . . . the best

mentors at this stage were especially warm and supportive. 'Perhaps the major quality of these teachers was that they made the initial learning very pleasant and rewarding. Much of the introduction to the field was as playful activity, and the learning at the beginning of this stage was much like a game."[lxxx]

Later, as Duckworth's quote suggests, our exploration and the mentor's role in our journey toward excellence transitions to a role of encouraging specialization. This is done through playful activity, warmth, and supportiveness, letting that exploration occur and then supporting success and interest in the mentored person. Find what they like and then support it. Find what moves them.

The next stage is to assist with practice. Here, the mentorship isn't just about encouraging the proverbial 10,000 repetitions "but also quality of time. Not just *more time on task*, but also **better time on task**."[lxxxi] As James Altucher says in Reinvent Yourself, if a mentor wants you to do things his way (during this process of encouraging practice), then "That's fine. Learn HIS way. Then do it YOUR way. With respect.

Hopefully nobody has a gun to your head. Then you have to do it their way until the gun is put down."[lxxxii] Here the two phases of self-disciplined practice are clear. First, discipline yourself to the standards of your master and mentor. Then self-identify with the task and learn to do it better.

Once you get those 10,000 meaningful repetitions in, the role of the mentor changes again. In this final stage the best practice for mentorship is to create a relationship where the mentor serves as a sounding board and a moral compass. The mentor is useful here because the stages of self-development toward excellence proceed like so: "most people first become attracted to things they enjoy and only later appreciate how these personal interests might benefit others . . . to start out with a relatively self-oriented interest, then learn self-disciplined practice, and, finally, integrate that work with an other-centered purpose."[lxxxiii] The mentor in this last stage, by providing a sounding board and moral compass, helps guide us out of self-disciplined but self-interested practice toward a direction that has moral relevance and purpose. The mentor helps us align our efforts with a goal so that our work has moral velocity and not just wasted speed.

While occasionally one person might fulfill all these various roles of mentorship — like a long-term figure-skating coach who spots a talented skater, drills that skater for the years required to become a champion, and then serves as a guide when later in life the skater takes on a role herself as coach, or announcer, or establishing a skating school — it is more common by far to have different mentors who satisfy differing requirements as we grow, learn, and mature.

Here's one such case:

> Former president Bill Clinton remembered his grandparents and a college professor who taught him the importance of American values as important figures in his life. But it was Nelson Mandela, he says, who gave him the best advice he ever received. "He came out of twenty-seven years in prison a stronger, greater man than he was when he went in," Clinton wrote. "He said his transformation began when he realized his tormentors could take everything from him

'except my mind and my heart. Those things I would have to give them. I decided not to give them away. And neither should you.'"[lxxxiv]

Here, Clinton suggests that it was his grandparents and a college professor who first encouraged him and then helped him along the road of practice toward understanding the values he would use as his guide. They encouraged his interest in politics and Americana. They mentored him in the values that would propel him to office. But, later, meeting and getting such advice from Mandela, Clinton used the compass and encouragement Mandela provided to reaffirm his own beliefs amid his own trials and tribulations. Like Mandela, Clinton was encouraged to continue his support and his interest in, his advocacy for, American values because they weren't things that could be taken away. Clinton's grandparents and professor served mentoring roles in the beginning and middle stages of Clinton's life. But Mandela stepped in, later, as a moral guide and, although not stated, probably as a sounding board too.

This leads to one last aspect that a mentor can help with.

We all stumble. We all fall down along the way. Clinton certainly stumbled while he was in office, only to return to public life conducting work on behalf of his foundation and campaigning for his wife and for various other causes.

The realization that it is not just a matter of facing setbacks but also of surviving actual falls, spills, upsets, and the like, made Angela Duckworth change the way she thought about her "Grit Scale." This happened when one of her study subjects said, "I don't like that item [on your survey] that says, 'Setbacks don't discourage me.' That makes no sense. I mean, who doesn't get discouraged by setbacks? I certainly do. I think it should say, 'Setbacks don't discourage me for long. *I get back on my feet*." [lxxxv] What's more important, for our discussion of mentorship is that this same survey subject said she "almost never got back up all by herself. Instead, she figured out that asking for help was a good way to hold on to hope." [lxxxvi]

The actor James Earl Jones provides an anecdote about getting pushed, or – in this case – prodded, back to one's feet and then using that experience to overcome an obstacle. He recalls a teacher of his named Professor Crouch who discovered Jones had a stutter. Jones writes of this professor:

> He questioned me about why, if I loved words so much, couldn't I say them out loud? One day I showed him a poem I had written, and he responded to it by saying that it was too good to be my own work, that I must have copied it from someone. To prove that I hadn't plagiarized it, he wanted me to recite the poem, by heart, in front of the entire class. I did as he asked, got through it without stuttering . . . my confidence grew as I learned to express myself comfortably out loud.[lxxxvii]

Without a little push to stand in front of class, face and surmount his stutter, would James Earl Jones have gone on to be the voice of Darth Vader or the writer from Field of Dreams (among so many other acting highlights?) We can't know. All we can judge, here, is that Jones ascribes some of his success to this incident, this push from a mentor at a time when he very well may have lost hope.

The final stage of mentorship is to become a mentor yourself. This stage doesn't necessarily need to be sequential. We all master things, or aspects of things, at different stages. Someone can come along and be instructed and inspired by us, by our skills and by our approach to problems or to life, without our ever feeling as if we have attained some heightened state of mastery.

Take my old boss as an example again.

Did he think he had it all figured out? Sometimes he certainly acted that way. But now that I've been in his shoes, I think not. He was probably bluffing. He was probably uncertain of his decisions, just as I am uncertain of many of the decisions I've made while in increasingly influential roles. Yet, even unwittingly, that man became something of a mentor for me.

In becoming a mentor we only really need three things: a certain perspective or experience (even if it is very new and skin-deep, it still might be useful); a willing subject, whether that person directly approaches us to engage in a process of formalized coaching or merely observes us from a distance; and the willingness, ourselves, to devote some of our time, energy, and effort to giving back.

As Charles Bukowski writes, "You begin saving the world by saving one man at a time; all else is grandiose romanticism or politics."[lxxxviii]

CHAPTER 9
Realism

In this chapter we're going to discuss realism in the context of leading a life empowered by Stoic principles and Stoic virtues. Some of the basics we've covered already, such as the importance of stopping and thinking about what is *realistically* under our control and how to make our efforts more fruitful by concentrating on those things that are, truly, realistically, controllable.

But we're also going to take this a step further. Or, actually, several steps further. (Otherwise, why have a separate chapter at all to cover this topic, eh?)

The emphasis here will shift to realism in the context of parsing truth from what is often a confusing miasma of circumstances, of situations that are not black-and-white, and of our own human difficulty in achieving objective perception. However, it is good to remember why we're doing this. It isn't just a thought experiment. It isn't just an academic debate about how unknowable reality can be, how difficult it can be to separate objective truth from subjective perception. All that academic chit-chat is fine and good. But when theories connect to the purpose of facilitating our ability to understand what situations we control and what situations we do not control (and the correlation that follows with where to direct our precious time and effort) then we arrive at and refine strategies for how to go about living well, now, in this world. That is the advantage of pursuing a Stoic philosophy of life: living well. Living virtuously.

And living virtuously means living realistically.

So, onward to the problem of how to achieve a realistic perspective.

Groucho Marx is a good starting place here. He famously said, "Who are you going to believe, me or your lying eyes?"

He meant this as a joke. But at its heart the problem with perception is one we deal with daily, even if we're not always aware of the struggle with *misperception*, the very high rate of misperception we as humans experience (and then project outward from ourselves in our dealings with the world.) For example, one article on crime and testimony quantifies this by explaining that, although eyewitness testimony is often a deciding factor in court cases (and is viewed as very reliable by juries and judges alike), in fact the misperceptions inherent in eyewitness situations make such testimony the least reliable type, often contradicted by hard evidence.[lxxxix] What does this say about our preferences as humans and our thirst for realism? It says that we judge another's perception, regardless of proof to the contrary, as more true and more real than actual fact.

This is a problem.

It's a problem Stoic thinkers have contemplated and written about.

Ryan Holiday, in The Obstacle is the Way, says, "Outward appearances are deceptive. What's within them, beneath them, is what matters. We can learn to perceive things differently, to cut through the illusions that others believe or fear. We can stop seeing the "problems" in front of us as problems. We can learn to focus on what things really are."xc

This gets after the issue of external perceptions and how important it is to think about the world in terms that are objective and realistic. We base our decisions on those external perceptions. We base our judgment, if we're acting in a Stoical manner, on how much these external events can be brought under our personal influence and control. So developing an awareness of our limitations in perceiving things correctly, and then using that time-honored pause, that tranquility, to try to pierce the veil of imperfect perception, all of this goes a long way toward making better choices.

But that's the external piece. There's the other half of the equation too: learning to think about ourselves, our desires, and our perceptions of ourselves, in an equally objective and realistic manner. Seneca comments on the well-tread Stoic tradition of applying realism to the process of thinking about our internal selves when he says:

'A consciousness of wrongdoing is the first step to salvation.' This remark of Epicurus' is to me a very good one. For a person who is not aware that he is doing anything wrong has no desire to be put right. You have to catch yourself doing it before you can reform. Some people boast about their failings: can you imagine someone who counts his faults as merits ever giving thought to their cure? So—to the best of your ability—demonstrate your own guilt, conduct inquiries of your own into all the evidence against yourself. Play the first part of prosecutor, then of judge and finally of pleader in mitigation. Be harsh with yourself at times.[xci]

The process of harshly investigating the self, its motivations, and its perceptions of the world leads to self-awareness. It seems like putting yourself through such a process might be a terrible (or at least a very deflating) torture, a difficult thing to do to yourself on a daily basis. Again, here comes that old idea of Stoicism being a dour, un-fun way to lead live. Yet, self-realism, and the pause of reflecting on the self and on our ability to perceive both ourselves and the world around us can actually be joy enhancing as well as useful.

Take, as an example, one of the Stoic techniques for responding to insults. This technique doesn't actually require specific self-knowledge or specific knowledge, objective knowledge, of the world at large. But it does rely on those things, on flawed external perception and clear (or at least modestly clear) self-perception, to build up an armor of humor as your defense.

Epictetus explains the technique: "If you hear that someone is speaking ill of you, instead of trying to defend yourself you should say: 'He obviously does not know me very well, since there are so many other faults he could have mentioned.'"[xcii]

Without specific self-knowledge, this technique works just fine. Just use that line. Paraphrase it. It'll get a laugh and diffuse the situation, turning the table on the person who slighted you. But you could also make your response more specific if you've developed a more objective level of self-awareness. For instance, if someone makes a comment about you that isn't fair (or realistic even), combat that by actually pointing out a few of your specific faults. This is Epictetus' technique but applied to a specific self-awareness and self-knowledge that will be sure to win points with co-workers, subordinates, even family. Say something like, "Yeah, he (or she) says I'm weak at doing paperwork. True enough. But if he was really watching he'd see that I'm also really bad at talking to people, nervous, full of stage fright, and never should have been hired as the PR Director for this firm at all." People will laugh at that, especially if you've actually been doing well and leading a great PR team while making good (or even fair-to-middlin') speeches. The modesty and humility and the grains of acknowledgment and self-awareness inherent in that type of response are traits that co-workers and friends will appreciate and find endearing.

As David D'Alessandro says in Executive Warfare: "Organizational leaders, like politicians, have to prove their humanity – or at least that they are not so divorced from reality that they can't recognize good work when they see it."[xciii] By demonstrating and reflecting criticism in a way that is humorous and self-aware, rather than by being combative or defensive, we open ourselves up to shared suffering and the type of vulnerability that builds trust.[xciv] We show our friends and companions and co-workers that they can expect humor and humility from us in tough situations. This is a good thing and a corollary benefit of applying the razor of realism to our speech, our actions, and our leadership.

Let's take this even one level deeper and talk about Socrates and Columbo.

Yep. Famous philosopher Socrates. And Columbo, that 1970's sitcom detective guy.

As unlikely as it might at first seem these two figures share some commonality in the way that they understand themselves and use the human element of misperception among their audiences to unearth truth.

As Tim Delany and Tim Madigan explain in their book "Lessons Learned from Popular Culture," the character of Columbo –

> . . . so ably performed by actor Peter Falk. His filthy raincoat, his disheveled hair, his nagging wife, and

his forgetful nature were all part and parcel of a beloved iconic figure. The **Columbo** episodes, as fans will recall, were not typical "who-dunnits." Instead, we the viewers knew from the beginning the identity of the murdered . . . The fun was anticipating how detective Columbo would find out "who dunit" and trap the murdered into confessing. In most cases, the arrogant killers underestimated Columbo's investigative prowess. By "playing dumb" he lulled them into a false sense of security. They would give him vital clues without realizing it. Columbo's most irritating technique was to leave a room and then return, with a befuddled look on his face. Scratching his head, he'd say "Just one more thing . . ." and ask a seemingly innocuous question. The killer, by then eager to see the last of this annoying fellow, would quickly answer, but would later find out that the question was not so innocent after all, when Columbo returned to say "You're under arrest."[xcv]

Columbo used the suspect's misconceptions, that willingness to judge a book by its cover, to his own advantage. This underscores not only the importance of looking more deeply into the book itself (as these murderers failed to do, glancing only at the surface shambles and the bumbling actions) but also reveals how influence perception of those around us. This isn't a call to purposefully contrive a different character, a façade to present to the world in order to fool it into believing something untrue about you. Rather, it should reinforce an awareness of the same situation Epictetus describes in his method for parrying away insults: 'if only you knew how bad I really am at x, y, or z.'

In short, be aware that the reality you believe people see probably isn't actually their perception. Like Columbo, you can use that to your advantage if need be. But first, before you can harness it in any way you need to drive your own realization, your own realism, deeper in analyzing and knowing yourself and the world around you.

So how does that relate to Socrates, I hear you asking from afar.

Well, as Delaney and Madigan say,

> In many ways Columbo was a modern version of Socrates. Socrates too was known for his unkempt appearance, his nagging wife Xanthippe, and his distracted way of acting. But more important . . .

there are many similarities between Columbo's detective techniques and Socrates's method of discovering truth. Both were polite but persistent and while people with nothing to hide usually enjoyed their company, those who did not wish to have their alibis or ignorance probed would react in exasperation or with violent threats to both men. Suddenly, Socrates would no longer seem such a befuddled character.[xcvi]

Socrates used his outer persona to lower the expectations of those with whom he debated. He did not want to approach them with answers in hand, but instead to elicit answers and derive philosophy and truth by leading the dialogue, by pulling truth from those he engaged with. He may have already perceived the realness he sought, the truth he sought, but he hit his interlocutors with a double-whammy: his own illusion of ineptitude falling away just at the same time the truth he was leading them toward made its appearance from behind the veil of misperception.

Both Columbo and Socrates gained enough self-awareness to allow them to manipulate how they appeared to others. By causing others to dig through misperceptions and trip over those misperceptions, they each revealed truth. This is good insofar as truth is good.

But there remains yet another level of realism in the Stoic pursuit. That of developing an ability to discern good from bad. How else to live well, to live the 'virtuous life' that Stoicism calls for, if the faculty for knowing good hasn't been developed?

Oddly enough, though, the place to start when you seek this level of realism isn't in creating labels of 'good' and 'bad.' The place to start involves applying a different sort of discernment altogether. (This very much parallels the way that negative visualization at first seems **negative** but then, later, opens up realms of positive appreciation and gratefulness we probably hadn't contemplated before.)

Here is how Epictetus describes this particular application of realism: "Does a man bathe quickly (early)? Do not say that he bathes badly, but that he bathes quickly. Does a man drink much wine? Do not say that he does this badly, but say that he drinks much. For before you shall have determined the opinion, how do you know whether he is acting wrong?"[xcvii]

What Epictetus encourages us to do is to delay the judgment call. For us to once again take a moment, slow down, (maybe seek tranquility), and separate ourselves from the urge to label an action good or bad. When we do this we give ourselves time to see the action for itself and not embroil that action in emotional baggage, in assertions that might not have any bearing on objective fact. While bathing or drinking wine are Epictetus's examples, the premise holds for all decision-making. Step away. Calm down. Try to see the action and maybe also the second-order effects of that action for what they are, minus labels lumping that action into good or bad categories.

It might be helpful, even, to substitute the word 'value' for 'good' or 'bad.' This allows us to create a distinction and perhaps even layers of value that don't tie themselves up with a judgment call. The value can adhere to different levels of being, to different needs. And we can then sort through those layers, unemotionally, or less-emotionally, and find better ways toward truth and success, better ways around the things that seem like obstacles in our lives. Value, for instance, might be in the simple cost of a product at the super market. Or it might be in the freshness and nutrition of that product. Those are two different scales of value, both operative at the same time, but by examining them each independent of calling a certain vegetable 'good' or 'bad' you'll be able to arrive at an objective decision that isn't clouded by an initial subjective opinion.

Irvine explains this in an evolutionary context when he writes, "We can use our reasoning ability to conclude that many of the things that our evolutionary programming encourages us to seek, such as social status and more of anything we already have, may be valuable if our goal is simply to survive and reproduce, but aren't at all valuable if our goal is instead to experience tranquility while we are alive."[xcviii]

When we do this two-step dance – first moving away from subjective calls like 'good' or 'bad' and seeking better understanding of actions for what they are, and then, second, replacing the judgment terminology with 'value' measurements and thinking – we allow ourselves to see things more realistically and react to them in more productive ways.

To develop an increased capacity for realistic thought, we first must look at the world outside us and try to become objective about our perceptions. We then turn that objective capacity on ourselves (perhaps building up a keen defense against insults along the way). We can use this newfound realism and self-reflection to build trust and empathy, shared understanding, with friends, loved-ones, and co-workers, opening up realms of vulnerability that we'd been afraid to admit to before. And then, in achieving greater self-awareness, we can lead others – like Columbo or Socrates did – toward more clearly perceiving the world and more clearly understanding us (which produces a favorable reaction in those with good intentions, and a more visual, visceral reaction in those who would otherwise hide their motives and desires). All of this is good. Couple it with the strategy of replacing subjective valuations (terms like 'good' and 'bad') with objective assessments based on value – even better: value directed at things we can control – and we will increase our effectiveness in the world.

Like wider tires on a racecar, which touch more asphalt and give greater traction, we will thereby be able to interact with the world and with those around us in a more realistic, productive, and rewarding way.

CHAPTER 10
Agility

When I worked at Macmillan Publishing I went through quite a number of "re-orgs" and, as a consequence, an ever-changing array of bosses and supervisors. The first few times this happened the process stressed me out. I was fearful. I had trouble adjusting. Then, as I learned to accept the situation instead of complaining, I realized I had to get good at adjusting and adapting to these new situations because the newness and the change would be a normal and continuing part of my work environment. Such change wasn't going to go away. So I had to embrace it.

As I did that, as I altered my perception and my attitude toward the never-ending stream of change, I began to see wider benefits to being adaptable and agile. I became personally less stressed, and I also started to add a lot of value to the organization by preparing myself and equipping myself to succeed and to do what was necessary no matter what new regime took the reins around or above me.

The process of change, and the cultivation of a posture of adaptability, meant that I didn't have an 'old way of doing things' to which I could become attached. As a consequence I began, along with others on my team, to use the change to make incremental, iterative improvements. Each disruption created an opportunity for growth. Each obstacle became part of the path we would take to succeed. We stayed loyal to our bosses (whoever they might be at any given time) but we also made sure we did not become too parochial. We kept the other departments on our side, did not make enemies of them, because we never knew if − a month or a year or a week from any given day − we'd soon be working with, under, or through them once the next reorganization occurred.

I learned not to take good situations for granted.

I learned not to get down on myself, or my team, or my work place, when things got tough.

I learned that difficulties could be turned into advantages.

And I taught myself the lasting benefit of agility.

I think this quote from Robert Greene's "The 50ᵗʰ Law" really sums up what I learned during that time of shuffling and changing and never-quite-feeling-settled at Macmillan – the sense that, at first, I was struggling with the chaos but then, later, that I learned, grew, and came through the process stronger and better. Here's what Greene has to say:

> You too face a world full of obstacles and limitations—a new environment where the competition is more global, complicated, and intense than ever before. Like the hustler, you must find your freedom through the fluidity of your thoughts and your constant inventiveness. This means having a greater willingness to experiment, trying several ventures without fear of failing here or there. It also means constantly looking to develop new styles, new directions you can take, freeing yourself up from any inertia that comes with age. In a world full of people who are too conventional in their thinking, who respect the past far too much, such flow will inevitably translate into power and more room to move.[xcix]

Let's examine these qualities more closely and better map them against their Stoic underpinnings.

A good place to start, when looking for Stoic commentary on agility, happens to be in the darkest and most bleak circumstances. These might be different from our modern complaints about job reorganizations and so forth, but the principles at work transfer across the ages and the issues. One such issue, back then, that we no longer really need to overcome now days, was the problem of exile. Seneca was exiled for 8 years to the island of Corsica. During this time he wrote to his mother the letter now called "Consolation to Helvia." His purpose was to convince her not to grieve for him – he, the one who had been wronged and sent away, was working from the inside out to cheer up his own mother! The ending of Seneca's letter demonstrates how he turned the tables on the situation of exile through a simple trick of the mind. He wrote:

> I am as joyous and cheerful as in my best days:
> indeed these days are my best, because my mind is
> relieved from all pressure of business and is at
> leisure to attend to its own affairs, and at one time
> amuses itself with lighter studies, at another eagerly
> presses its inquiries into its own nature and that of

the universe: first it considers the countries of the world and their position: then the character of the sea which flows between them, and the alternate ebbings and flowings of its tides; next it investigates all the terrors which hang between heaven and earth, the region which is torn asunder by thunderings, lightnings, gusts of wind, vapour, showers of snow and hail. Finally, having traversed every one of the realms below, it soars to the highest heaven, enjoys the noblest of all spectacles, that of things divine, and, remembering itself to be eternal, reviews all that has been and all that will be for ever and ever.[c]

Seneca's trick here was to **not think** of exile as a punishment but as an opportunity. He rejoiced, he literally says he was 'joyous and cheerful,' in the circumstances of his exile because those circumstances freed him from the cares of his position advising Emperor Nero. He could turn his mind to other pursuits, exploring the world, the lands, the oceans, the cosmic and natural phenomena around him, even the divine. This he welcomed as a change from the pointedly dangerous and Byzantine lifestyle he was forced to lead in Nero's court.

Although it might at first seem ostentatious to compare my situation at Macmillan with Seneca's exile on Corsica, the exact same mental gymnastics worked for both of us. Where Seneca had to rethink his mindset regarding exile, I had to rethink how I approached the constant reorganizations and chaos. In each of these situations benefit could be found: the space and time to explore and the opportunity to hone skills of agility. We were both faced with situations that could have made us buckle. Instead we not only persevered but found ways to turn the problematic issues into advantages.

Here is the underpinning to agility – that very same Stoic approach to problem solving. Change ways of thought rather than trying to change circumstances. Thought, at least your own pattern of thought and perception, is fully under your control. Circumstances, even embedded in the grammar of the word, are peripheral and not under your control. They are the things that "stand around you." It is your choice whether to perceive such surrounding things in a way that makes them appear to be walls or appear, instead, to be bridges.

The theme of changing perspective Seneca hits time and time again. Perhaps most simply, he framed it thus: "Cicero [who was also exiled] called himself a semi-prisoner, but really and truly the wise man will never go so far as to use such an abject term. He will never be a semi-prisoner, but will always enjoy freedom which is solid and complete, at liberty to be his own master and higher than all others. For what can be above the man who is above fortune?"[ci]

Freedom is omnipresent, as long as we are willing to define it correctly: freedom within the bounds of what we control. In that space, that freedom, we can be agile. And creative.

As we discussed in our earlier chapter on fearlessness, the development of agility is important because it is key ingredient to creativity.

Agility + Fearlessness = Creativity.

How simple is that?

It's awesomely simple as long as we approach it from the perspective advocated by the Stoic philosophers. Don't look for freedom in the circumstances that surround you. Find freedom via rethinking the problem. In that freedom, where you change your outlook on the problem to focus only on those things you control, you will find agility. You'll be left exiled on an island as punishment and, instead, be the comforter and the philosopher and the discoverer of new things because you have the time and the space and the mental clarity to devote to ideas you'd never otherwise have the capacity to think about. Likewise, if you're in a stressful work environment, where the rules and the organization itself change day-to-day, you can find the opportunity to develop the same sort of agility, treating it as a chance to learn better team-working, better adaptability, better endurance.

In that situation, once the space / freedom has been created within you (and from there, extending outward, also around you); you have your opportunity for agility.

But *opportunity* needs to be emphasized.

All the opportunity in the world could be present but without then attacking the problem in a fearless way, you might sense a creative possibility but never actually motivate yourself to create. Hence the two concepts work in tandem. Create space, recognize it as freedom, allow yourself to be agile rather than rooted, and take that fearless leap.

Bruce Lee talks about this state, likening it to water. He says,

> Be like water making its way through cracks. Do not be assertive, but adjust to the object, and you shall find a way around or through it. If nothing within you stays rigid, outward things will disclose themselves. Empty your mind, be formless. Shapeless, like water. If you put water into a cup, it becomes the cup. You put water into a bottle and it becomes the bottle. You put it in a teapot, it becomes the teapot. Now, water can flow or it can crash. Be water, my friend.[cii]

In this quote he covers everything we've discussed: the pause (not being assertive upfront, letting it happen); the mental agility (getting rid of that rigid exterior and understanding that you control your own shape, rather than the exterior shapes of cup, bottle, or teapot); and then the fearlessness, the crashing or flowing, that motion forward into and around a problem. Bruce Lee's formula represents an active, in-the-moment style of Stoicism.

But agility does not need to be as serious as either Seneca or Bruce Lee make it out to be.

There's a good story from Africa about a dog, a leopard, and a monkey.

The dog is loping along, thinking he's in charge of life, on top of the world, when he notices, much to his dismay, the approach of a leopard.

Boom. He's in trouble. He's going to get eaten. The food pyramid out there on the savannah doesn't have dog (or human for that matter) at its apex.

So the dog looks around. He's not going to change the food pyramid. He's not going to suddenly grow bigger muscles or faster reflexes or sharper teeth and become an apex predator so that he can fend off a leopard. But he can control the way he thinks about the problem.

He spies a pile of bones. He goes to them, sits down, and starts gnawing on part of the old carcass. With his back bravely turned toward the approaching leopard, he waits until the moment before the leopard springs before he says, "Boy, what a delicious leopard. I hope another one comes by so I can have my fill for dinner."

This makes the leopard pause and reconsider. He says to himself, "Wow, what a crazy devil dog. I don't want to mess with him."

And he leaves.

That's good agility. Life-saving agility. And no small measure of fearlessness either. The agility (reframing the problem of not being the apex predator) and the fearlessness the dog demonstrates by acting on that agile solution, prove to be his salvation.

But there's another part to the story.

A monkey has been sitting in a tree watching all this go down. The monkey thinks he sees an advantage for himself. Why not get the mean, king-of-the-animals leopard on his side? So he swings through the branches until he catches up to the leopard.

"Hey leopard," he says. "That dog was just pulling your leg. Those are some old bones he found. He never killed a leopard."

The leopard is furious at being duped. So he invites the monkey to climb on his back. Off the two go to confront the dog and show the dog who is really boss.

The dog again sees this coming. Again, he's terrified. He knows, unless he does something, he'll surly be killed and eaten. But like water he pours himself into the shape of this new vessel. He fits his mental state to the new circumstances rather than trying to overcome the circumstances themselves by fighting or running away.

As the monkey and leopard approach the dog waits until they're within earshot and then says (still not looking in their direction), "Boy, I wish I knew where that monkey went to. I sent him off a half hour ago to find me a new leopard to eat and he's still not back."[ciii]

By fitting his position to the situation, by fitting his mental state to the problem, rather than the other way around, the dog turns the tables. He finds the creative solution to his (very dire) predicament. And he does this twice. He finds success and then he capitalizes on that success, iterating his initial solution toward an even better product.

There are some lessons we can capture from the dog's agility.

First, there is no direct link to 'talent.' Just as in the sections on hard work and perseverance, where effort counts twice as much as talent on the road toward building skill and achievement, here talent figures not at all. Never did the dog's talent for deception come up as a prerequisite of his salvation. Or, if it does figure, that equation looks something like this: skill in being agile = talent (a baseline ability) x effort. This is the same formula that Angela Duckworth propounds in

her book "Grit" for the development of any skill.[civ]
Where agility is a skill, honed through a process of
trial, error, and retrial like that which I experienced
during my time at Macmillan, then creativity is, itself,
a product of the application of effort once again.
Creativity is the achievement in this situation. It is the
water flowing through the cracks, or crashing when it
needs to. It is: *effort* (once again, but now we might
call it 'fearlessness') x *skill* (at being agile) to take that
leap into producing, or equaling, *creativity*.

Like the dog, you might be preserved by this
creativity.

Like Seneca, you might turn what could be a bad
or boring or demeaning situation into joy.

That's the power of creativity.

As Victor Frankl wrote, "Man does not simply exist
but always decides what his existence will be, what he
will become the next moment. By the same token,
every human being has the freedom to change at any
instant."[cv]

The source of that change, the same source from which so many Stoic precepts flow, is the ability to know and act on those things we as humans actually control.

Even during his harrowing time as a POW, James Stockdale exercised this discernment between controllable and non-controllable. He explains perhaps better than anyone how this liberated him to be creative and to solve problems when almost all freedoms had been taken from him. Note how the bolded text demonstrates his application of controllable and non-controllable circumstances and how that produced creativity in his leadership:

> Against the backdrop of all the posturing and fumbling around peacetime military organizations seem to have to go through, to accept the need for graceful and unself-conscious improvisation under pressure, to break away from set procedures forces you to be reflective, reflective as you put a new mode of operation together. I had become a man detached – not aloof but detached – able to throw out the book without the slightest hesitation when it **no longer matched the external circumstances.** I was able to put juniors over

seniors without embarrassment when their wartime instincts were more reliable. This new abandon, this new built-in flexibility I had gained, was to pay off later in prison.[cvi]

This is powerful stuff. It is joy inducing, perspective altering, goodness bringing, and problem solving. It is the sort of key that not only fits the lock of many, if not most of our dilemmas, but altogether makes the lock disappear. Creativity and the agility and fearlessness needed to produce the achievement of creativity; these things turn locks into ladders.

PART III: Soul

CHAPTER 11
Being Authentic

The free soul is rare, but you know it when you see it - basically because you feel good, very good, when you are near or with them.   Bukowski

We can be fearless. We can develop our agility (and many other skills) through effort and perseverance. We can teach ourselves to look at problems differently. We can learn that true joy comes from the tranquility of living well, of living virtuously. And we can discover the power of making decisions from within that tranquil place inside ourselves, and how that tranquil place can help us hone our ability to work hard and persevere as the arrow of our moral compass points toward goodness and eliminates waste.

These are the steps that make up the stairway of a Stoic lifestyle. They are important. And they will take you on a journey of self-discovery and self-improvement, a journey we have charted in the first two sections of this book.

But let us not forget the ground floor from which this staircase rises.

The self.

In this coming section, we'll examine the self in more detail. We'll look at authenticity through a Stoic lens. We'll work on learning from and using the past as a teacher. We'll remind ourselves that the nature of being human is a social nature and, more importantly, we'll discover that the Stoics never intended us to be anti-social. They want us to embrace the good things in life, albeit in moderation. And then we'll recap the whole purpose of living a virtuous life when we discuss gratefulness.

So, onward into an exploration of the soul.

Onward to look into what 'soul' and 'self' mean.

We're talking about that exact 'self' with whom, inside of whom, you inescapably must make all decisions, take all turns, enjoy all the great moments and endure all the hardships of this journey. That self represents the raw material the Stoic lifestyle will hone.

That self represents the initial input of 'talent' in Duckworth's formula for achievement, the raw nature you bring to the table and then refine through effort to get to the place where you can say you possess skill, and then, with more effort, refining yourself again, you turn that skill into achievement.

The self is your baseline, your ground floor.

The self is my baseline too, my ground floor.

Same for all of us.

It's a thing we must embrace and around which we must array the tools of Stoic behavior in order to help **ourselves** become all we can be.

As the long, arduous, joyful journey of Stoic learning and improvement unfolds before you, it is wise to return for a moment and think about yourself. It is wise to reflect on who you are and how you can be a more authentic you. Let the self shape your efforts. Let it shine through your skills and achievements. Let it be the basis for your virtue. And stay true to it. Because authenticity is a key to freedom, a key to tranquility. We've mentioned it time and again, here, in this book, just as it is mentioned in many other writings on the subject of virtue and Stoicism: the fact that tranquility is both the object of a virtuous life and the way to give yourself time, and mental clarity, in the individual moments of decision-making that lead toward goodness. Authenticity produces that tranquil state. Happy and balanced and with your exterior and interior selves aligned with one another, you become tranquil. You reach that pinnacle of joy.

Furthermore, authenticity, both ***being*** and ***showing*** others who we are in our deepest selves, is a prerequisite for developing the bonds of trust and influence with others that help us become successful members of communities. In other words, authenticity helps us extend the reach of what we can control and influence, beginning from just our internal perceptions, then extending to effect and control our own actions, and then – via influence developed in authentic behavior – to effect friends and associates around us.

Brené Brown comments on this in her Ted Talks
about vulnerability. She says:

> Authenticity is a collection of choices that we have
> to make every day. It's about the choice to show up
> and be real. The choice to be honest. The choice to
> let our true selves be seen.[cvii]

And, later, she adds:

> Because true belonging only happens when we
> present our authentic, imperfect selves to the world,
> our sense of belonging can never be greater than
> our level of self-acceptance.[cviii]

Here we receive a formula for not only being true
to ourselves but also for gaining traction in the world
around us, a way to wrap our metaphorical wheels
with chains, like driving on an icy road, so that on the
roadway of life we gain a little leverage, a little better
advantage on the slippery surface (never fully in our
control) of how others see us and how we can effect
them. By starting inward, with the self, and then
making the minute adjustments to our behavior Brown
suggests in her 'collection of choices,' we begin to let
our inner truth, our authentic selves, shine through for
who we are. We do not present our friends and

colleagues with one face, then save a different face for other endeavors, or for ourselves. Unified, the world around us − which is always going to get a vote on how it perceives us − will see and be able to judge a consistent human. If the choices we make are good ones, virtuous ones, then the world will see and judge and respond to consistent goodness.

This is powerful.

Showing up and being real makes people respond to us. It creates belonging. We get buy-in from those around us. In belonging to a group, or to an array of groups in different facets and times of our lives, we participate in and effect the direction and effort of the group and thereby extend our ability to have at least a small amount of influence over otherwise uncontrollable circumstances. In proportion to our authenticity to ourselves, achieved by constant adjustment and choices that make us show up and be real, we influence others.

Now, the goal here shouldn't be "authenticity for the sake of controlling others." That's conniving and, of course, blatantly inauthentic. The goal is to live well and achieve tranquility. Putting effort against things we control is just one way to focus on decisions that lead to tranquility. Authenticity extends the sphere of that tranquility and will be seen as a boon, as a consequence we will become that 'feel good' person Bukowski says others will notice when they're 'near or with them.' Authenticity is a way to bring the tranquility of the virtuous life, the Stoically virtuous life you decide to lead, into the sphere (and perhaps also the service) of others.

Lest we think this is all modern pop-psychology mumbo-jumbo, lets return to Epictetus. He says something very similar to Brené Brown:

> When you have decided that a thing ought to be done and are doing it, never avoid being seen doing it, though the many shall form an unfavorable opinion about it. For if it is not right to do it, avoid doing the thing; but if it is right, why are you afraid of those who shall find fault wrongly?[cix]

Epictetus takes a bit harsher viewpoint than Brown; or at least his words come through with an iron will behind them. Rather than advocating the force of good you project into others' lives via your own authenticity, he suggests that the 'right' thing be done regardless of external forces. Still, in doing so, the idea of rightness extends from us. We set an example. And, though over the short term we might aggravate those around us who cannot see the rightness in our actions, our self-conviction and steadfast assurance in pursuit of goodness will, over the long, increase respect and gain the same sort of traction that belonging to the group creates. Think about friends and coworkers: who do we admire more, the sycophant who does whatever the boss or the group wants, or the maverick who holds to an ideal of rightness and sets the example for others no matter what the personal cost may be? Looking at a person from this light, we can see that Epictetus' model of behavior and Brené Brown's advocacy for letting the true self show through our actions are one and the same. The principle of authenticity creates a climate of trust, admiration, and influence that – when aligned with virtue – cannot help but benefit those whom it touches. At different times, varying from circumstance to circumstance, you might find your influence creates Brown-like vulnerability and belonging or incites, at least initially, Epictetian aloneness that only later morphs into respect and gratefulness.

But does Epictetus always require a practitioner of Stoic virtues to be authentic to himself and to rational precepts, even when, for instance, others around him are being irrational?

No.

Although he is sometimes faulted as being without sympathy for others, Epictetus actually prefers to make the practice of authenticity more difficult by putting us in a strange position with regard to those who show irrational emotion. He writes:

> So far as words, then, do not be unwilling to show him sympathy, and even if it happens so, to lament with him. But take care that you do not lament internally also.[cx]

While this does much to refute the idea that Stoicism, and especially Epictetus, frown on the idea of sympathy in general, this statement also seems, at first blush, to advocate purposeful dishonesty.

However, if we look at this again through the Stoic lens, through the lens of making decisions based on what we truly can and can't control in our lives, then Epictetus' method makes better sense. We can control our internal life. We can't control someone else's reactions or emotions. Because of this Epictetus wants us to be authentic to each of these different situations separately, even if they happen at the same time. Internally, he wants us to be authentic to our Stoic pursuit, to wall off the external influence of the unnecessary or irrational emotion and preserve our internal tranquility. Externally, he advocates for us to engage with other people. He doesn't want us to be or to act without the human element of sympathy for our fellow men. He wants us to walk a line between genuine sympathy, even outward displays of emotion, while inwardly we preserve our calm.

This can be a difficult balancing act. It is certainly a balancing act that requires us to be mindful, to go back to what Brené Brown says – "authenticity is a collection of choices." This means being mindful. And *mindful,* remember, means that we take the same tranquil pause and then make a unemotional decision about how to react to things in order to be our most authentic selves and to direct our effort against those things that we can control.

The case of the artist Banksy, a modern figure who plays with and challenges notions of authenticity, seems to offer some further enlightenment on the challenges and standards we face when trying to navigate this "collection of small choices."

Banksy made his name through "outlaw spraying [of graffiti] – or, as the argot has it, 'bombing' – of walls in Bristol, England, during the 1990s" and has since gone on to produce art that "commands hundreds of thousands of dollars in the auction houses of Britain and America."[cxi] Because of this outlaw nature of Banksy's early art and his self-confessed run-ins with law enforcement over that art, Banksy keeps his true identity a very closely held secret. This has created some mystique, a benefit. But it is also a challenge in terms of authenticity, not only for him as a person and an artist, but also for his work: *is a piece of graffiti an actual Banksy original or not?* The work often shows up in cities around the world: Detroit, London, Paris, Singapore. How do his fans know if it is original or copy-catted?

Banksy, in his usual provocateur style, resolves these issues through interesting means. First, he has set up a foundation cheekily named "Pest Control" to vet and authenticate his art. This arrangement also:

> . . . protects him from prying outsiders. Hiding behind a paper bag, or more commonly, email, Banksy relentless controls his own narrative. His last face-to-face interview took place in 2003. While he may shelter behind a concealed identity, he advocates a direct connection between and artist and his constituency. 'There's a whole new audience out there . . .'' Banksy has maintained. 'You don't have to go to college, drag 'round a portfolio, mail off transparencies to snooty galleries, or sleep with someone powerful, all you need now is a few ideas and a broadband connection. This is the first time the essentially bourgeois world of art has belonged to the people.[cxii]

Banksy controls his ability to appear in public. His choice not to be seen or to become a public figure himself allows him to create mystique, sure, and it allows him to avoid legal issues too, but it also presents a thorny problem for him on the authenticity level. He resolves this by adding the counterculture edifice of an 'authenticity' foundation, his "Pest Control," as well as direct advocacy for art itself as the means by which to establish the sort of authentic contact that others often adheres to the person (like in the case of Andy Warhol, for instance). Once art leaves his direct control, Banksy knows he can no longer influence it. He can't worry about it. But he can use it as a way to engage. In fact, it could be argued that the whole point of his art, or of any art, is to extend the authenticity and the opportunity for engagement between the artist and the audience and that the cult of personality interferes with, rather than improves, the authenticity of that engagement.

In true Stoic form, Banksy takes a liability (his reluctance to appear in public) and turns it into a benefit. His way is the way of Bruce Lee's water, fitting itself to a mold shaped just like Banksy himself. A mold shaped in an authentic format.

One last bit of Epictetus should be brought up in the context of authenticity. Here, the Stoic master seems to again support authenticity over the sort of fearlessness and agility we've discussed earlier. He seems to suggest that it isn't actually wise to apply the sort of effort, fearlessness, and agility that can be used to 'punch above our weight' and overcome obstacles – even though we've highlighted those very things as some of the great benefits to a Stoic lifestyle.

On this topic Epictetus writes:

> If you have assumed a character above your strength, you have both acted in this matter in an unbecoming way, and you have neglected that which you might have fulfilled.[cxiii]

This quote places rails against falsity in how we portray ourselves. It therefore advocates authenticity. But rather than asking us **not** to try in our goals and pursuits of big things, what it is really doing, I believe, is once again asking us to take a big problem and break it down into manageable portions. It asks us to tackle things we have developed the skill to tackle. It asks us to do those things authentically and perhaps in sequence, building toward mastery and larger objectives. It asks us not to neglect the small tasks that, in sum, build toward greater things.

What this statement decries is the situation where we might falsely claim to have achieved large things, grandiose things, at the expense of fully analyzing the whole set of circumstances to scope the situation into its controllable and uncontrollable bits. And then to attack those bits, even if they are not glorious, one at a time. In summary, to achieve authenticity in our actions we must:

- Approach each controllable circumstance in an authentic manner.
- Put aside uncontrollable things.
- Show compassion and empathy, even in situations where we know another person hasn't acted rationally, or worries about things out of their control.

- Endeavor to separate our controllable internal reaction from the benefits of commiseration and human belonging that come from helping others through their (irrational) griefs and their (perhaps unfounded) joys.

At one and the same time authenticity allows us to be vulnerable and armored against the challenges of the world. It's a complicated situation, but one where mastery can provide tangible benefits in both the creation of our internal tranquility and in the way people around us see and react to our actions. Through constant small, virtuous choices, we become consistent and an influence for good.

This isn't an easy thing. But nothing really wonderful ever is.

Of the vulnerability and the armor of authenticity, Tyrion Lannister from Game of Thrones may say it best when he lectures Jon Snow:

> Never forget what you are, for surely the world will not. Make it your strength. Then it can never be your weakness. Armor yourself in it, and it will never be used to hurt you.[cxiv]

CHAPTER 12

The Past as Teacher

I'm going to indulge myself for a moment and quote in its entirety one of my favorite passages from Stoic philosophy. This selection touches a chord in me because of the beauty of its language and also because of the depth of its thought. I challenge you to read it not just once, but twice, and to think about what it really says. Perhaps interpose a moment of silence, of tranquility, to let your mind absorb it. See if it embeds itself more deeply in you as a result.

The following passage provides a great lead-in to this chapter as well, since its primary goal is to show how the past should be considered and employed in the pursuit of a life based on Stoic principles. Although we cannot control the past (and therefore should not worry about it) we must use the past as the underpinning that informs and supports our decisions and our very being at the moment when we have the capacity to choose virtue over vice, the moment of 'now' when we can strive, improve, and control certain aspects of our existence. Without the past, without a reverence for and a deep grounding in where we have been and what we have done, we live merely a succession of moments. The pursuit of Stoic virtue requires more from us than that.

Without further ado, here is how Seneca teaches us to think about and utilize our past:

> Life is divided into three periods – that which has been, that which is, that which will be. Of these the present time is short, the future is doubtful, the past is certain. For the last is the one over which Fortune has lost control, is the one which cannot be brought back under any man's power. But men who are engrossed lose this; for they have no time to look back upon the past, and even if they should have, it is not pleasant to recall something they must view with regret. They are, therefore, unwilling to direct their thoughts backward to ill-spent hours, and those whose vices become obvious if they review the past, even the vices which were disguised under some allurement of momentary pleasure, do not have the courage to revert to those hours. No one willingly turns his thought back to the past, unless all his acts have been submitted to the censorship of his conscience, which is never deceived; he who has

ambitiously coveted, proudly scorned, recklessly conquered, treacherously betrayed, greedily seized, or lavishly squandered, must needs fear his own memory. And yet this is the part of our time that is sacred and set apart, put beyond the reach of all human mishaps, and removed from the dominion of Fortune, the part which is disquieted by no want, by no fear, by no attacks of disease; this can neither be troubled nor be snatched away – it is an everlasting and unanxious possession. The present offers only one day at a time, and each by minutes; but all the days of past time will appear when you bid them, they will suffer you to behold them and keep them at your will – a thing which those who are engrossed have no time to do. The mind that is untroubled and tranquil has the power to roam into all the parts of its life; but the minds of the engrossed, just as if weighted by a yoke, cannot turn and look behind. And so their life vanishes into an abyss; and as it does no good, no matter how much water you pour into a vessel, if there is no bottom to receive and hold it, so with time—it makes no difference how much is given; if there is nothing for it to settle upon, it passes out through the chinks and holes of the mind.[cxv]

Isn't that lovely?

Also, what does Seneca actually tell us to do?

He wants us to look backward, whether or not we are proud of and reconciled with our past. He wants us to embrace the past not because it is something we should rejoice over – although it is immune to the turmoil of the present, or the worry of future times – but because it is the vessel into which we pour our now. He wants us to take a pause during the now and situate our actions, our thoughts, and our desires in the context of who we are and where we have been. And he wants us to recognize and enjoy the fact that the past is immutable, rather than feeling regret over what we have done or have failed to do.

All these things are wonderful. And, in a way, they are like a counter-melody or an accompanying harmony to go along with the Stoic idea of negative visualization.

Powerful, isn't it?

Think about the future in its worst-case dimension. And thereby rob it of its ability to cause you too much worry.

Think about the past in its immutability and its freedom from want, from care, from hunger, from debilitation. And thereby rob it of its ability to make you feel regret.

Both, then, become tools for making better decision in the now.

Just take that pause. Let yourself visualize the worst case of the future. Let yourself remember the worst case of the past. Locate yourself, locate the vessel of yourself in the context of your personal, unchangeable past. Free yourself from regret over anything you've done but use that past to hold the present, to shape the present. Use the past to affect the things that can be affected. Other things: let them go. And don't worry about everything. What's the worst that can happen? Negative visualization, at its ultimate end, tells us the worst is death. But death is natural, out of our control. It is rational. We've already discussed it, how we should not fear it but instead use it, use our mortality, as the impetus for living more virtuously while we have time.

Peering back into the past, unlike negative visualization (which asks us to use our imagination to project forward in time), allows us to draw on situations we have survived, challenges we've overcome, and lessons we've learned. And those experiences – viewed through the lens of memory – should come to use all at once, with an easiness and a lack of pain (once we wash away the sense of whatever regret we might irrationally hold). In this way, the past serves as a secondary tool, a reinforcement of negative visualization.

Let me explain this through a real-life example.

A couple years back I had a very important presentation to give for a project I was working on at graduate school. Public speaking in front of many, many people.

Like most of us, I was worried how I would do. I worried over not only the fear of speaking in such a forum, but the project was also important to me and I wanted to do well. I wanted to do the subject justice. Everyone else in my grad school cohort seemed to be very natural speakers but I knew I would have trouble. I worried about how I would perform for days and weeks leading up to the event.

Long story short, I messed it up.

I stunk.

Failed.

Stumbled on words, forgot material, came across cold and stiff.

I could have thought of this as the end of the world (and, for a hot moment I did!) But, was it? Looking back from my vantage point today, I know it certainly wasn't. I've got that graduate degree. I've gone on to a successful career. That episode is now ancient history.

More importantly, I jumped back in again just a few weeks later and gave public speaking another go. That time I did a little better. I spoke again a few weeks after that. Better still. My classmates supported me. I kept trying. The humiliation, fear, and failure from the first attempt started to fade and I was left with

– I still am left with – a series of impressions, getting up to the podium, shuffling my notes, clearing my voice, starting out with a joke that failed or succeeded, all of this trial-and-error that led, slowly, toward improvement.

Now I'm much more comfortable in front of large audiences.

I developed a skill. Remember our equation? Skill = talent (of which I had only the smallest amount to start) x effort (which I was willing to put into this situation).

Today, when I give a presentation I remember how hard it was to overcome my fears and my inexperience but I also know that even the worst performance, the rock-bottom most terrible job I could do, was and is conquerable.

That's an important lesson. It's one I take with me from my personal history.

And it's a lesson that ties the idea of "The Past" to the idea of "Fearlessness."

We make decisions now based on how we've challenged ourselves in the past and to what extent we've learned our capacity for grittiness over time. We become fearless by filling our days, by building our vessel, our reservoir of history, with experiences that create a capacity for fearlessness.

Angela Duckworth, in her book Grit, offers a recipe for this, one she has used to teach her own children how to be grittier, more fearless and persevering. Her process, she says, "both requires grit and at the same time builds it."[cxvi]

She calls this process "The Hard Thing Rule" and it goes like this (parents or adult mentors must comply AND participate):

1. Everyone has to do a hard thing.

2. You can quit, but not until the season is over, the tuition payment is up, or some other natural stopping point has arrived.

3. You get to pick your own hard thing.

Basically, Duckworth creates a forcing mechanism to develop grit. She makes her children accumulate experiences that teach them to persevere and also build the capacity for perseverance. They face fears one at a time. They face challenges one at a time. But, by doing so, they build up a history of this behavior. They shape the vessel into which Seneca says we pour our days and our individual moments. That's how the capacity for grittiness can be developed, simply by being gritty. Simply by setting an intention and putting into practice certain events (no matter what those events might be, right? The kids get to pick!) aimed not so much at the individual skill involved in the 'hard thing' but at the overall forming of the vessel of our past experience. The overall capacity we have for looking back into our past and saying to ourselves, 'Hey, whatever I'm facing now just ain't so bad. I can do it.' That's grit.

One other important point to talk about from Seneca's big quote.

The small things.

He mentions how they tend to fade away over time. He very beautifully says that the small things seem to disappear, that we are "put beyond the reach of all human mishaps, and removed from the dominion of Fortune." These things, these small things, were once the wants, fears, and attacks of disease (Seneca's examples) that caused disquiet. At the moment these small things happened, back when they occurred in the present, they loomed large. But looking on them later, from a historic perspective, from the vantage point of memory, they fade in importance and seem almost to disappear away completely. Once that happens, once those things fade, the resulting rosy (at least rosier) past is fixed and firm and immutable and can "neither be troubled nor be snatched away."cxvii

Our meditation on the past becomes a method to achieve what Marcus Aurelius calls for when he discussed our fixation on 'the small things.' He writes, "A key point to bear in mind: The value of attentiveness varies in proportion to its object. You're better off not giving the small things more time than they deserve."cxviii

The past naturally winnows away the important things from the unimportant things. By thinking through similar situations that occurred before – like how failure at speaking in front of a large crowd wasn't actually the end of the world (for me or for millions of other nervous public speakers!) – we bring to bear that powerful tool, much like negative visualization. We ask ourselves, 'What's the worst that *actually happened?*' Rather than 'What's the worst that *could happen?*' Same exact principle, except here, the passage of time has stripped away a lot of the extraneous baggage, those 'small things' that might cloud a negative visualization of the future. Marcus Aurelius asks to put the small things in their place. The past makes that happen without too much effort on our part, as long as we're brave enough to put our regrets aside and look at our personal histories from an objective viewpoint, a learner's viewpoint. A Stoic's viewpoint.

Although significantly more morose in its outlook, Seneca provides a link between the past and future, how past and future merge together, or should merge together, to make us appreciate, activate, and immerse ourselves in the present moment. Despite its sadness, the following passage has value as a piece to meditate on just in the same way the opening quote does. Use the words below as motivation to first take a moment of contemplative calm, of tranquility, in your decision-making. And then to recommit to living a Stoic lifestyle, so that you might turn the fears of the future into well-intentioned, fearless, virtuous effort in the present moment. That's the way to live a good life. That's the way to create a past filled with only the sort of small regrets and failures that help us iterate toward success.

Seneca says:

> So I would like to fasten on someone from the older generation and say to him: 'I see that you have come to the last stage of human life; you are close upon your hundredth year, or even beyond: come now, hold an audit of your life. Reckon how much of your time has been taken up by a money-lender, how much by a mistress, a patron, a client, quarrelling with your wife, punishing yourselves, dashing about the city on your social obligations. Consider also the diseases which we have brought on ourselves, and the time too which has been unused. You will find that you have fewer years

than you reckon. Call to mind when you have ever had a fixed purpose; how few days have passed as you had planned; when you were ever at your own disposal; when your face wore its natural expression; when your mind was undisturbed; what work you have achieved in such a long life; how many have plundered your life when you were unaware of your losses; how much you have lost through groundless sorrow, foolish joy, greedy desire, the seductions of society; how little of your own was left to you. You will realize that you are dying prematurely. [cxix]

Rather than dying prematurely, use your past – your memory and history, your regrets and successes – to inspire the present. Live now. Live well. And know that the past is there for you, inside you, as a vessel that shapes your present, if you have the strength and patience to slow down, face time, and let the lessons of your life inform your now.

CHAPTER 13
Sociability

Live, love, laugh, leave a legacy.   Stephen R. Covey

Critics often fault the Stoics for not advocating for us to enjoy life. In fact, as we've mentioned earlier, the very term 'stoic' conjures images of miserly behavior, Scrooge-like emotional isolation, and an emphasis on enduring pain and deprivation rather than enjoying life. That image comes from reading only half the Stoic formula for a good life. It's very much like a modern news report: the sound bite on Stoicism might be factually correct, but it misses the context, it misses the fullness of what the Stoics recommend. It takes the gloomy part and forgets the warmth promised not only by the achievable, in-the-now goal of bringing about tranquility, but also the recommendation, the requirement, that Stoic philosophers give to their practitioners to be part of the world and – wonder of wonders! – to enjoy the human elements of being and belonging.

For proof of this, let's return to Seneca's description of the good life. He writes:

> The happy life, therefore, is a life that is in harmony with its own nature, and it can be attained in only one way. First of all, we must have a sound mind and one that is in constant possession of its sanity; second, it must be courageous and energetic, and, too, capable of the noblest fortitude, ready for every emergency, careful of the body and of all that concerns it, but without anxiety; lastly, it must be attentive to all the advantages that adorn life, but with over-much love for none – the user, but not the slave, of the gifts of Fortune.[cxx]

It's this last part that really pops for me. And it should pop for you too (also, I'll mention, this last part should have flavored the image of Stoicism through the annals of time, rather than its glum, endure-against-all-odds image). Let me reiterate this portion. The Stoic, Seneca says, "must be attentive to all the advantages that adorn life, but with over-much love for none."[cxxi]

There's the key.

Seneca has issued a call for us to enjoy life.

And he's done that at the same time he reminds us to strive for balance and non-attachment.

Seneca wants us to put tranquility to the forefront but not to block out sociability, fun, and the other advantages and good things life can bring. But what are these advantages and good things?

For one: our social interactions and the joy they can impart in our lives and in the lives of others in a symbiotic way, as we engage with and spread the love. That's a first advantage of being social.

As William Irvine says, in a Guide to the Good Life, the Stoics weren't against sociability or fun at all. They just urged some caution, and wanted us to keep our tranquility as priority numero uno. Irvine says, "They [the Stoics] thought that man is by nature a social animal and therefore that we have a duty to form and maintain relationships with other people, despite the trouble they might cause us."[cxxii]

Here, we see, the concept goes a little further than just encouraging sociability. Because our human nature is social, our relationships aren't optional. They're a duty. In other words, having human relationships isn't something we control. We don't get to choose to have absolutely zero relationships. Even if we pursue hermit-like seclusion, meditation, and withdrawal from the world, we all were born into the world, nurtured, raised, taught, loved, chided, molded, formed, and made into the people we have become through a series of interactions, of relationships, with those who have loved, challenged, and mentored us. Even in the most stringent seclusion such relationships carry on inside us. The effects remain. The memories remain. And so we have no choice over having or not having relationships. They are a duty. They are omnipresent. They are part of the inescapable fabric of being human.

What can we do then?

Just like when we confront any other 'problem,' the Stoics advocate breaking this one down into its component parts, those that are controllable and those that aren't. What is controllable in our relationships? For one, our attitude toward them. We can choose how to approach other people. We control our own mindset toward others.

Vin Diesel provides a really loving, well-thought anecdote about his mindset toward other people partway through a recent interview he conducted with Maria Menounos. Vin, as many of his fans know, spent a long time working as a bouncer at a mega-nightclub. There he'd have to constantly deal with all kinds of problematic behavior, people being obnoxious and showing their worst sides. Of this experience, he said:

> Once, after a big fight, just another day at work, [I was] bummed about the fact I was just doing this job after all this time, was feeling like why is this my daily life to suppress or check everyone's anger at this giant 10,000 person nightclub. My father was there and he said, 'You know Vin, I've traveled all over this world . . . and I've realized something: **people by and large are good people.**' This sounded pretty simple and yet it meant so much . . . if you believe that in your heart – and not everybody watching this can say that or is ready to

say that or is comfortable enough with themselves enough to say that – if you really believe in your heart that people by and large are good people, it affects the way that you address the world. Post in and post out [speaking of his social media presence] I address a world that I feel, in my soul, is comprised of good people.[cxxiii]

Vin chose to look at people differently. He chose to start addressing people in a way that assumed some qualities of inherent goodness. He chose to look at the situation and control the part of the situation that was, for him, controllable: his own attitude. He couldn't prevent people from fighting. He couldn't make them stop their obnoxious behavior. But he could shield himself (and his tranquility) from some of it and he could approach the problem different by changing his own internal start point. Vin Diesel continues to use this viewpoint to inform his approach and he implies that it not only helped him overcome his anxiety and depression about where he was going in life and why he was doing what he was doing at that stage when he worked as a nightclub bouncer, but he also suggests he continues to use this approach because it causes a reciprocal effect: other people react to him differently when he approaches them looking for (or assuming) goodness.

That's awesome.

And, based on Stoic principles for living virtuously, this assumption of goodness seems to be a pattern of behavior that will produce similar results for others who adopt it. It's not just a Vin Diesel success story. It's not Vin Diesel mind control. Now, we might not end up with the same results as Vin Diesel. We might not star in the next installment of Fast & Furious or be asked to voice the next Groot character in Guardians of the Galaxy, but in ways little and big our (controllable) choice about how we view others almost certainly will make them view us differently.

Ryan Holiday speaks about this in his book "Obstacle is the Way." It's of course a basic tenet of his (and of Stoic philosophers in general) that we should look at obstacles as opportunities. We should turn obstacles upside down and use them to our advantage. [cxxiv] In just this way, the natural tendency to "hang onto bad things" in relationships is preventable AND its exorcism from our thoughts and actions can be one of the ways we turn the obstacle upside down. By releasing the bad things, by forgiving and forgetting, we not only cleanse our minds and help return the equilibrium of tranquility to our daily being (thereby allowing us to make better, more rational decisions), but we also demonstrate clemency. We reset relationships and poise ourselves for an increase of enjoyment and goodness rather than bracing for a cycle of retribution and continuing anger. Vin Diesel doesn't say this directly, but we can imagine him returning to the same mega-nightclub the day after, or maybe the week after his father provided the insight that seems to have changed Vin's life. Vin is trying to put this advice into practice. He's trying to give people the benefit of the doubt. He's trying to see the good in them rather than always preparing himself for the next fistfight by viewing everyone in the nightclub as having suspicious intentions.

Perhaps this causes Vin to get blindsided a few times, caught flat-footed when someone out-of-line tries to take a swing at him.

But, perhaps also, his initial reaction of trust, of looking for good, of being calm (and the concurrent increase of internal tranquility that improves his decision making), causes a few people to stand down, a few angry customers to 'not take that swing.' This benefits Vin. It benefits the customers. It benefits the nightclub. And it might even rub off on the other bouncers.

Imagine it: a whole nightclub of good-spirited, Zenlike bouncers and patrons who, while they might have come looking for a fight, find themselves gazing into Vin's eyes and seeing there the combination of calm, forgiving rationality and the underlying willingness to kick drunken butts. That's potent. Catching. Viral. And maybe it contributed to Vin Diesel's success.

There's another aspect to this too, though.

We can see it in Vin's relationship with his father.

We can maybe hypothesize that it manifested between Vin and his fellow-bouncers or between Vin and his customers.

It's called the "social multiplier effect" and its important in understanding what Seneca termed as the 'duty' we have in maintaining positive, enjoyable, fruitful social interactions. This multiplier effect builds on the case that sociability isn't something we get to choose. It does away with the notion that we should ever retreat to that mountainside, find ourselves a cave, and abscond from humanity and human interaction forever. Not only are we born with and unable to avoid the imprint of sociability (thus making it a moot point, an uncontrollable point) but we also directly benefit from sociability.

The social multiplier effect was understood as far back in time as Confucius, who said, "Never contract friendship with a man that is not better than thyself."

This jives with the more modern theory about how we, as growing, evolving people, should consider ourselves the product, or average, as motivational speaker Jim Rohn says, of the "five people we spend the most time with."[cxxv] If we choose (and this choice is imminently controllable) to spend the majority of our time with five lousy people, we ourselves will be lousy.

If we choose to spend the majority of our time with five people who intrude on our tranquility, we'll never achieve true tranquility. If, on the other hand, we consciously seek and cultivate friends and fellow travelers on this journey of life who are awesome, who inspire awesomeness, and who carry within them the seeds of tranquility, thoughtfulness, and joy, we will increase our quotient of those qualities. We will become more tranquil, more thoughtful, and both more filled with joy and more enjoyable to others.

We will become awesomer!

The social multiplier effect, while observed and commented on by philosophers like Confucius since time out of mind, was described in a more scientific manner by James R. Flynn. He noticed this first in observing children play basketball and he used the same logic to explain generational changes in abstract reasoning (whoa). His observation, in short, was that:

> By getting better, each kid inadvertently enriched the learning environment for the kids he or she was playing against. Because one thing that makes you better at basketball is playing with kids who are just a little more skilled.[cxxvi]

Applied more broadly, as the 'generational changes in abstract reasoning' experiments confirmed, this means that not just in basketball, but in all other facets of our ability to learn (and enjoy) life, the people we surround ourselves with matter.

If we surround ourselves with better students as friends, we become better academically.

If we surround ourselves with more loving individuals, we increase our capacity to love and to enjoy love.

If we surround ourselves with better athletes, our skills on the court, or the field, or the ice rink improve.

And if we surround ourselves with bouncers willing to look first for the good in people, then we not only diffuse situations that could become violent, but we actually increase the number of good people, acting in good ways, and the overall amount of goodness in a place — even a place as fraught with violence and bloodshed as the front entrance (or back alleyway door) of a mega-nightclub.

In short, as Irvine says, the Stoics advocate social engagement, but "they warn us to be careful in choosing our associates; other people, after all, have the power to shatter our tranquility – if we let them."cxxvii

Fun is good.

Being social can create fun.

It relaxes the mind. It increases our tranquility. We shouldn't shy away from it. We should in moderation and balance enjoy the 'advantages that adorn life.' But we should always keep in mind that we control certain factors of these interactions. We can't completely do away with human relationships. But we can choose who we interact with and how we shape those interactions.

We see this shine through in Marcus Aurelius's famous quote, his famous exhortation to himself about reframing his perceptions of the people he will meet during the course of his normal day's work ruling the Roman Empire. He told himself:

Begin each day by telling yourself: Today I shall be meeting with interference, ingratitude, insolence, disloyalty, ill-will and selfishness – all of them due to the offenders' ignorance of what is good or evil. But for my part I have long perceived the nature of good and its nobility, the nature of evil and its meanness, and also the nature of the culprit himself, who is my brother (not in the physical sense, but as a fellow create similarly endowed with reason and a share of the divine); therefore none of those things can injure me.[cxxviii]

But this isn't all Marcus had to say on the subject.

As Irvine explains:

Even when other people don't do anything to us, they can disrupt our tranquility. We typically want others – friends, relatives, neighbors, coworkers, and even complete strangers – to think well of us. We therefore spend time and energy trying to wear the right clothes, drive the right car, live in the right house in the right neighborhood, and so forth. These efforts, however, are accompanied by a degree of anxiety: we **fear** that we will make the wrong choices and that other people with therefore think poorly of us." This might seem to imply that we should be hermits, but Marcus Aurelius says "fellowship is the purpose behind our creation." Thus a person who performs well the function of man will be both rational and social.[cxxix]

If there exists a better coupling of the rational and the social, of the need for mindfulness and the need for intimate and experiential joy, I haven't found it. People can be bad. But we must choose to see the good and to approach the world with goodness in our hearts, because that interaction, that moment when we put ourselves forward in fellowship, is the actual purpose of why we are here on earth.

I hope that you take this forward with you – Vin Diesel, Marcus Aurelius, Seneca, and Flynn's Social Multiplier Effect – and use it to reframe your approach to joy, to fun, and to bonding with others. Be mindful about it. Be balanced. Surround yourself with goodness and be a source of goodness and light for others. But also know that the interactions you have, and how you frame those interactions, are one of the true advantages that adorn our lives.

CHAPTER 14
Gratefulness

It is more necessary for the soul to be cured than the body; for it is better to die than to live badly.
Epictetus

The quote above brings to mind one of the best scenes from what I think is surely one of the best movies of all time: Fight Club.

This is the scene where Brad Pitt's character, Tyler Durden, takes the gas station manager Raymond Hess hostage, forces him to his knees in the back alley behind the station, and puts a gun to Raymond's head while the narrator, Jack, stands in the background and almost writhes with discomfort. Tyler Durden looks berserk. He's already done plenty of manic, but strangely logical things (in a paradigm-shifting sort of way), like making soap from discarded human fat stolen from the waste bins of a liposuction clinic. We in the audience think Durden is going to execute Raymond. Jack thinks Durden is going to execute him.

Most importantly, Raymond too thinks he's going to die.

But just then Durden starts getting philosophical. He asks Raymond what he wants to be. Raymond confesses. He's lost the urgency over time, but once, before, he had dreamed of becoming a veterinarian. Durden takes Raymond's driver's license and lets him go, warning him that he'll be checking up on him in six weeks and if he hasn't taken serious steps toward becoming a vet, he'll follow-through with the execution threat.

Only after all of this finishes does Edward Norton's character, Jack, reenter the argument. He says, "This isn't funny. What the #*%@ was the point of that?"

To which Durden of course has an answer: "Tomorrow will be the most beautiful day of Raymond K. Hess's life. His breakfast will taste better than any meal you and I have ever tasted."

Jack then narrates directly to us in the movie audience, saying: "You had to give it to him. He had a plan."

This scene is pure Stoicism, an absolute exercise in negative visualization (taken to its extreme).

It's also an example of the strong and mutually reinforcing bond between negative visualization and the subject of this chapter – the subject which really forms the core of the **goodness** toward which Stoicism strives – our ability to live in a state of gratefulness.

Durden's application of this principle is illustrative, if a bit insane. It strikes at the heart of the issue, that same curing of the soul and the importance of the soul in comparison to the body that Epictetus wrote about. Both Tyler Durden and Epictetus are saying, *If the soul isn't in good shape, then what use is the body?* Durden just takes things a bit farther and threatens the body in order to convince the mind and the soul to live closer to an in-the-moment gratefulness.

That tool – though rarely if ever taken to the point of holding a weapon to someone's head – is the same tool Stoics use to encourage gratefulness and repair the damage that normal living can and does do to our souls and our ability to enjoy life. Negative visualization makes us slow down and savor what we have. The by-product of that savor is gratefulness.

William Irvine, in his book *A Guide to the Good Life,* describes the damage that comes when we don't live in a state of gratefulness:

> We humans are unhappy in large part because we are insatiable; after working hard to get what we want, we routinely lose interest in the object of our desire. Rather than feeling satisfied, we feel a bit bored, and in response to this boredom, we go on to form new, even grander desires . . . psychologists Shane Frederick and George Loewenstein have studied this phenomenon and give it a name: hedonic adaptation.[cxxx]

This is the explanation for ungratefulness, where it comes from, what it does, and how it sneaks up on us. None of us sets out to be in that state. Yet, the accumulation of stuff – things and achievements and the simple passage of time – tends to numb us, and (more dangerously) cause us to want more and more, to look beyond the now and beyond the things we have (and the things we control) toward distant shores that we do not control. We begin to worry about those things and forget the here and now. And the cycle simply loops over and over.

Negative visualization helps us break out of that cycle.

As we discussed earlier, negative visualization gives us time to pause and to reorder our priorities. It lets us focus on what we can and cannot control: death, as I've said, is not controllable in the end, so the fear of it tends to dissipate upon rational study, upon forcing ourselves to visualize the worst possible scenario.

Repairing the soul can sometimes require us to hold a metaphorical gun to our own heads (and then also play the role of the lunatic ready to check up on whatever our progress toward a personalized 'veterinarian school application' may be). Negative visualization can take that nerve-wracking form. It can be taken to the extreme. It can project outward to our eventual demise and thus reduce all obstacles to their proper, probably far-less-significant, places.

But it can also start and end more simply and less threateningly, while still being effective.

There's a lovely Chinese children's story that calls out the links between this sort of less-than-life-threatening negative visualization and the production of a state of gratefulness. The story begins with a peasant family who work the fields for their living. They are very poor so most of their meals consist of a mixture of rice and fish, with dried fish being stored for the winters. The little girl in this story begins by hating this meal. She hates the taste of fish. It's too much of the same thing all the time. She longs for variety and meals fit for rich people. But one winter . . .

> . . . the snow came early and stayed for a very long time. Everyone had their stores of rice in sacks, kept safely away from rats and mice. Their dried and salted fish was hung high, near the ceiling . . . The rice was lasting out well, but the fish was nearly used up. Soon most of the meals were made from rice

alone. The fish was all but finished and then it was gone. [The girl] began to realize that she actually loved to eat fish. The rice was so plain without it. She complained to her mother. She said that she did not like to eat rice without fish.

Her mother came and sat beside her.

"Rice is very good for us. It keeps us alive. We must be grateful that we have rice to eat. Some people have no fish and no rice at all. How do you think they feel? They must be very hungry. We must be happy because we are not hungry."

"But I am tired of rice." the girl said.

"You must learn to control yourself and not complain about things that cannot be changed. You will just feel bad and make other people unhappy too. You do not want to make you father unhappy, do you? If he sees you smiling and eating your rice, he will be happy, because you are not moaning! He is grateful that we still have rice. He can smile about that and so can I. You must learn to smile about your plain rice too.[cxxxi]

This worked. The little girl, with some effort, learned to be grateful for the rice in addition to learning to appreciate (and be grateful for) the taste of fish when it was available.

But, in addition to this, later that same winter another family, whose daughter was a friend of the little girl, ran out of food completely. No fish and no rice either! They came and started to share the rice stored by the little girl's family. And this made the little girl even happier. What she realized through this process was a tremendous bounty of gratefulness, brought about by the experience of negative conditions (which is like Raymond's experience of Tyler Durden's threatened execution, not so much a visualization as an actual experience that drives home the gratefulness.) Once the benefit of the fish was taken away, it became much more palatable. The girl became much more grateful for its presence. Once the threat of death was in the air for Raymond as he knelt with Tyler Durden cocking the hammer back on his pistol, the possibility of life, and of living to fulfill an otherwise difficult personal goal, became much more palatable. Durden suggests that Raymond, as a result, becomes instantly grateful. He will love and enjoy his breakfast the next morning more than any breakfast before.

There are two additional and powerful points suggested by the combination of the Fish and Rice story's ending and the byproduct of gratefulness Durden claims that Raymond will feel. First, in the Fish and Rice situation, once the girl develops the internal capacity for gratefulness by realizing that the once-loathed taste of fish was something she, personally, wanted to appreciate and rethink, she was able afterwards to extend her newfound capacity for gratefulness on a broader and more abstract level. She felt grateful for sharing her rice, she might even have felt grateful for the opportunity to be personally deprived of rice, because it gave her happiness to help her friend and her friend's family eat and survive. The negative experience, tied to negative visualization, created first an internal gratefulness, and then, after having practiced this simple form of gratefulness, the girl developed the ability to increase her gratefulness. All of this taken together created happiness, joy, the very virtues Stoicism wants us to know and possess. In the same way, Tyler Durden says that the negative experience of the almost-execution. Tyler Durden claims the same thing happened for Raymond Hess. First he feels a gratefulness for living. And then that sense of gratefulness grows and can be applied to more abstract and distant concepts: how wonderful breakfast is (but then, one presumes, a bounty of additional gratefulness to boot).

Joy comes from gratefulness. And gratefulness can be built. This is the second powerful insight from these two stories. Gratefulness (and hence joy) can be created whole cloth, from scratch, via negative visualization. And then it can be increased in capacity and quality through practice. The continual exercise of our rationality (to apply negative visualization) and the production of a (tranquil) state in which we really encourage a grateful accounting of our life's riches together build our gratefulness ability (just as exercise builds muscle). The Stoic blog Prokopton discusses the habit of gratefulness:

> A regular commitment to being grateful can turn into a habit. Once this happens then day to day difficulties can be put into their proper context. Your outlook on life slowly starts to transform. It's

a small habit that sometimes you can forget to do. But it's worth the effort.[cxxxii]

So, you can start with negative visualization, make it a daily habit, and then, persevering and being gritty in the application of this habit, day in and day out, you can start to transform your outlook on life. You can take an initial talent (a first wee bit of gratefulness, like gratefulness for breakfast) and apply effort to that talent in order to help yourself develop the skill of being grateful. Then you can take that skill, put more effort into it over time, and that will result in achievement. The achievement at the end of this chain is joy, and perhaps also, success in life. What we have here is Angela Duckworth's formula all over again: effort x talent = skill and effort (again) x skill = achievement. It's the same principle. The same exact steps. It's just applied to the abstract idea that joy can be created through gratefulness.

Perhaps there is no better example of the dual nature of gratefulness as an achievement (joy + material success) than that which is evidenced by the life of Marcus Aurelius. His ***Meditations*** capture both the process of cultivating thankfulness and gratefulness in small and large ways daily, and the result of that process (success and enjoyment in life). These things are the achievements that gratefulness aims toward. They are the end state for Stoic virtue: the good life.

Looking closer, Marcus's ***Meditations*** can be read as a non-stop prayer to gratefulness, an expression of his appreciation for friends, teachers, family members and other people around him, helping him focus on what he can control (his mindset toward them). As the Prokopton blog says, "He was grateful for the help he received from others. This went towards shaping his character, offering opportunities for his education, and fostering his spiritual development."[cxxxiii]

I think these stories – Rice and Fish, Fight Club, and Marcus Aurelius – provide a pretty broad base of evidence for the effectiveness of gratitude. But we can take this even one step further. Now, through the miracles of modern science, we don't have to rely on subjective anecdotes.

Several scholarly studies on the correlation between gratefulness and well-being have been conducted (even though the researchers complain that "It has been well documented that psychology has been more interested in studying vice than virtue."[cxxxiv]) In one particular study, not only was there a strong correlation between gratefulness and subjective well-being, but the results pointed out that:

> Gratitude might promote happiness by enhancing one's experience of positive events, by enhancing adaptive coping to negative events, by enhancing encoding and retrieval of positive events, by enhancing one's social network, or by preventing or mitigating depression.[cxxxv]

A bit later the same study also suggested:

> Although we have demonstrated that gratitude can cause positive affect, it is still possible that happiness enhances gratitude as well . . . we support the notion that happiness and gratitude may operate in a "cycle of virtue" . . . whereby gratitude enhances happiness, but happiness enhances gratitude as well. This may be another "upward spiral" where positive affect has been proposed to provide benefits for the individual that tent to feed into further benefits.[cxxxvi]

So here, again, we see the benefits of gratefulness compounding. Scientific rigor in investigating the link between gratefulness and subjective well-being (a way to scientifically formulate the idea of 'joy') shows a strong link. What's more, the two things likely seem to work together reciprocally.

All of this means:

- We can learn gratitude (via negative visualization)

- We can broaden the scope of our gratitude (via practice)

- Once infused to sufficient degree, the result of the skill of gratitude is twofold: success in life (becoming a Veterinarian or being a kick-butt Emperor of Rome) and also joy

- As we produce joy (not as we find it external to ourselves but as we, internally, produce it) it could create an "upward spiral" that reinforces gratitude. Joy creates gratitude. Gratitude creates joy.

Sounds like an awesome problem to have!

All of this scientific stuff is the data, the hard fact, under what the Stoics have known for a very long time. As William Irvine frames it, the Stoic's technique of "negative visualization, rather than making people glum, will increase the extent to which they enjoy the world around them, inasmuch as it will prevent them from taking that world for granted."[cxxxvii]

Seneca, Marcus Aurelius, Epictetus, and Tyler Durden would agree!

I can attest to the transformative power of gratitude as well.

In my own life, I find myself practicing gratefulness daily. I no longer have to force myself to feel gratitude, but instead I take gratitude with me everywhere, even for mundane things: my pets, the fact that I have a home and shelter over my head, my health. And also for not very mundane things, like family. Instead of worrying about losing these things, I use gratitude to make sure I'm not taking them for granted. I use negative visualization to make sure I'm prepared for worst-case scenario. I also use it to ensure I appreciate the value of time and maximize it to enjoy the finer things in life. I do this when I spend time with my wife, when I play with my cat, when I walk into my home. I find that the more I do it, the more I pause and let tranquility wash around me as I send gratefulness out into the world, the better I get at it and the happier I am. I appreciate for friends and colleagues more. I'm less focused on slights and more capable of forming and enjoying true relationships. If I dislike someone continually, I just teach myself to avoid them (a thing I can control) instead of trying to fix a problem I can't control or make the relationship perfect.

I could go on forever.

I'm tempted to do so.

But I know I'm mortal, just as you are, and I want to get out from behind this computer screen, out into the world, where I can **be** a Stoic, where I can *live* the Stoic lifestyle like Cato the Younger, rather than just talking or writing about it.

In that lifestyle, I've found so much goodness that I needed to share it. I hope that this book provides a roadmap for you to follow, a ladder to climb, an "upward spiral" that breaks you out of the notion that Stoicism stands for gloomy endurance of the world. As you work on bringing this philosophy into practice, I know these things will prove fruitful for you:

✓ As you begin **Building Awareness of What Is and Isn't in Your Control** you'll feel less frustrated and you'll start to experience the results of focusing your efforts. You'll have a first taste of success that should leave you wanting more!

✓ Once the vigor of working only on the portions of problems you control begins to take hold, I believe you'll develop a reinforcing **Self-Discipline** that will keep you on-track.

✓ The rails of that track are the Stoic virtues. Chief among them is tranquility. When the tranquil pause begins to feel less foreign for you, the benefits of

What It Means to Live a Virtuous Life should start to unfold around you and enfold you, much like that Buddhist visual aid of a budding lotus. It is a prescription for living better in the here and now, unlike other creeds where virtue accrues in order to help a person reach some immortal hereafter.

✓ Pausing in tranquility should help you discover **Fearlessness.** You parse away things that don't matter, break tasks down into component parts. At that point fearlessness, or what would seem to be fearlessness from the outside, will seem a mere application of rationality.

✓ On the far side of any problem conquered through fearlessness, you'll discover new opportunity. This, again, might be another "upward spiral" as you realize your fearlessness helps turn **Setbacks into Opportunities**. And with each conquered setback, you grow the capacity for more fearless behavior.

✓ But sometimes the problem just doesn't resolve easily, no matter how fearless we might be. The solution: **Hard Work and Perseverance**, the hammer chipping away at rock and the sweat of heavy lifting.

These first few items are the Body of a Stoic lifestyle, the building blocks. Once you've incorporated them as natural and habitual parts of your life, then you can begin fine-tuning – starting with our analogy for where the 'Mind' of a Stoic should be honed.

✓ This begins with Stoic **Decision-Making**, which at its core involves our human rationality, the thing that distinguishes us from animals. Rationality allows us to make choices that might seem superficially gratifying but, in the long run, lead to goodness, joy, and tranquility.

✓ Stoics understand **The Importance of Mentorship** as we learn from others who have walked the same road and have turned similar setbacks into opportunities.

✓ Like wider tires on a racecar offering firmer contact with the road, the cultivation of **Realism** will allow you to interact with the world in a more meaningful and impactful way.

✓ Creativity and the **Agility** and fearlessness needed to produce the achievement of creativity; these things turn locks into ladders. Agility is like water fitting the shape of the vessel into which it is poured. And it is the rational choice to do things different when and if a problem can't be overcome with brute force or persistence.

The Mind portion of this book is designed to sharpen specific Stoic capabilities. The last part, though, where we discuss the 'Soul' of Stoicism, should hit home a bit more universally. In this area we talk about broad overarching concepts that were hinted at earlier but that, with further meditation and application, can enrich your Stoic practice (and your life).

✓ The first of these is **Being Authentic**. It's like a big 'duh'. Of course you'd be authentic. But the deeper understanding of this reveals that our vulnerability, rather than holding us back, more often serves as an armor and as a link to encourage trust and compassion in others. It's a way to lead and to *be*.

✓ We cannot escape our past. So we might as well use **The Past as Teacher**. The goal, like a stronger form of negative visualization, since it is based in our own, personal experience of things, is to help us live more fully in the now.

✓ Unlike the reputation Stoicism carries before it, the ancient philosophers never intended us to withdraw from the world or endure the world in a detached fashion. They want us to enjoy all the things that adorn life. This includes practicing **Sociability.**

✓ And then, to finish, we could have ended with platitudes about **Gratefulness** but that wouldn't be the Stoic way. Instead, we returned to science and rationality to show that gratefulness and joy work together in another "upward spiral" that mutually reinforces one another. Gratefulness produces joy. Joy produces gratefulness. And both of them thrive in and enrich the depths of tranquility you and your new Stoic lifestyle will have created in and around you.

My dearest hope is that you take a few steps on this path, try it out, and measure for yourself the benefits and the joys that come to you. May they bless you a hundredfold and may you experience, as I have, the tranquility and the fearlessness, the success and the joy of this most practical and momentous way of living.

Works Cited

[i] Stockdale, "Courage Under Fire," p. 14

[ii] Long's translation, p. 11.

[iii] Ibid, 22.

[iv] Irvine, p. 87.

[v] Adam Taylor, Washington Post, March 15, 2016
https://www.washingtonpost.com/news/worldviews/wp/2016/03/15/an-all-female-crew-lands-a-plane-in-saudi-arabia-but-they-cant-drive-from-the-airport

[vi] www.ted.com/speakers/amy_purdy

[vii] Irvine, p. 123.

[viii] Seneca, "Consolation to Marcia."

[ix] From https://michaelhyatt.com/it-is-as-you-chose-it-to-be.html

[x] Holiday, p. 44.

[xi] D'Alessandro, p. 11.

[xii] Irvine, 263.

[xiii] Meditations, IV.33

[xiv]
http://www.moneyaftergraduation.com/2016/01/04/why-you-should-practice-poverty summarizing Tim Ferris

[xv] On the Happy Life, XIV.2

[xvi] http://theweek.com/articles/450712/4-life-hacks-from-ancient-philosophers-that-make-happier

[xvii] Seneca, "On Anger," bk. III, sec. 13.

[xviii] McGonigal, p. 129.

[xix] Richard Stengel, "Mandela's Way" TIME Magazine, http://www.today.com/popculture/prison-was-mandela-s-greatest-teacher-wbna36087300

[xx] Ibid.

xxi Ibid.

xxii Stockdale, p. 13.

xxiii Stengel, p. 18

xxiv Ibid.

xxv

https://www.theguardian.com/world/2013/dec/06/
nelson-mandela-life-quotes

xxvi Stengel, TIME Article on "Mandela's Way."

xxvii Holiday, p. 31.

xxviii Discourses, IV.1

xxix Seneca, Costa trans, p. 31

xxx

https://en.wikipedia.org/wiki/Marcia_(wife_of_Cato_
the_Younger) (especially Colleen McCoullough's
interpretation of Cato's position re Marcia).

xxxi

http://www.artofmanliness.com/2008/02/24/lessons-
in-manliness-benjamin-franklins-pursuit-of-the-
virtuous-life/

xxxii Ibid.

xxxiii Meditations, VIII.50

xxxiv http://www.thirteenvirtues.com/

xxxv Ibid

xxxvi

https://en.wikipedia.org/wiki/Poor_Richard%27s_Al
manack

xxxvii http://www.thirteenvirtues.com/

xxxviii Irvine, 36.

xxxix Long's translation, p. 14.

xl Greene; 50 Cent. The 50th Law, p. 244

xli Holiday, p. 29.

xlii Irvine, pp. 97-98.
xliii Pressfield, "War of Art," p. 51
xliv To Marcia, IX.5
xlv On Tranquility, XI.6
xlvi Greene; 50 Cent. The 50th Law, p. 59
xlvii http://blog.visme.co/amazing-leaders-who-once-had-crippling-stage-fright-and-how-they-overcame-it/
xlviii Teddy Roosevelt, "Citizenship in a Republic," speech at the Sorbonne, 1910. http://design.caltech.edu/erik/Misc/Citizenship_in_a_Republic.pdf
xlix Meditations
l Holiday, p. 18
li
https://www.reddit.com/r/IAmA/comments/5smddl/we_are_stoic_indie_developers_creating_the_banner/
lii
https://www.ted.com/talks/amy_purdy_living_beyond_limits
liii
http://www.creativitypost.com/psychology/famous_failures
liv http://www.chopra.com/articles/break-on-through-a-meditation-for-overcoming-obstacles
lv Irvine, p. 73
lvi http://www.quotes.net/quote/16935
lvii Holiday, p. 78
lviii Greene. 50th Law, p. 212
lix Duckworth, p. 39
lx Greene. 50th Law, p. 212

[lxi] Ibid.

[lxii] http://www.notablebiographies.com/Mo-Ni/Newton-Issac.html

[lxiii] Greene, 50th Law, p. 215

[lxiv] Duckworth, Grit, p. 42

[lxv] Ibid

[lxvi] Ibid, p. 44.

[lxvii] Duckworth, pp. 216-217.

[lxviii] Ibid, pp.194-195.

[lxix] Seneca, To Helvia.

[lxx] Epictetus, "Discourses," I.xv. 2–3.

[lxxi] Meditations.

[lxxii] Duckworth, p. 64

[lxxiii] https://www.theguardian.com/lifeandstyle/2014/nov/14/how-to-avoid-monkey-trap-oliver-burkeman

[lxxiv] https://www.quora.com/How-powerful-is-the-brain-compared-to-a-computer

[lxxv] http://www.nbcnews.com/science/human-brain-may-be-even-more-powerful-computer-thought-8c11497831

[lxxvi] Greene; 50 Cent. 50th Law, p. 37

[lxxvii] Letters from a Stoic.

[lxxviii] These points elaborate on the substance of the article "Three Ways to Learn from a Bad Leader," by Jamie Chavez, published May 16, 2016 at http://www.rebeccabender.org/blog/2016/5/19/three-ways-to-learn-from-a-bad-leader

[lxxix] Executive Warfare, p. 63.

[lxxx] Grit, p. 107

[lxxxi] Ibid, p. 118

[lxxxii] Altucher, Reinvent Yourself, taken from
http://www.jamesaltucher.com/2015/10/reinventing
-yourself/
[lxxxiii] Grit, p. 144.
[lxxxiv]

http://www.csmonitor.com/Books/2012/0119/Natio
nal-Mentoring-Month-10-life-changing-stories-from-
celebrities/William-Jefferson-Clinton
[lxxxv] Grit, p. 194.
[lxxxvi] Ibid.
[lxxxvii]

http://www.csmonitor.com/Books/2012/0119/Natio
nal-Mentoring-Month-10-life-changing-stories-from-
celebrities/James-Earl-Jones

[lxxxviii] Bukowski, from the poem "Too Sensitive," Tales
of Ordinary Madness, p. 100

[lxxxix] Anderson, Tiffany, "Juror Misperceptions of Eye
Witness Evidence," University of Northern Iowa,
2015.
http://scholarworks.uni.edu/cgi/viewcontent.cgi?artic
le=1191&context=hpt
[xc] Holiday, p. 27.
[xci] Letters from a Stoic
[xcii] Epictetus, Enchiridion, 2nd c.
[xciii] D'Alessandro, p. 222.
[xciv] For more on the relationship between vulnerability
and trust, see Brown, Brené, "Listening to Shame,"
Ted Talk, March 2012,

https://www.ted.com/talks/brene_brown_listening_to_shame/transcript

xcv "Lessons Learned from Popular Culture," p. 34.

xcvi Ibid.

xcvii Long's translation, XLV, p. 39.

xcviii Irvine, p. 235.

xcix Greene, 50th Law. http://goodinfection.com/book-quotes-the-50th-law-robert-greene/

c To Helvia, XX.

ci Seneca, On the Shortness of Life, trans CDN Costa, p. 7-8

cii Bruce Lee, https://www.brainpickings.org/2013/05/29/like-water-bruce-lee-artist-of-life/

ciii https://www.gaudreaugroup.com/gaudreau-journal/the-dog-the-leopard-and-the-monkey/

civ Duckworth, p. 42

cv Holiday, p. 36

cvi Stockdale, p. 6

cvii https://blogs.psychcentral.com/imperfect/2017/04/inspirational-quotes-to-help-you-know-yourself-and-live-authenticity/

cviii Ibid

cix Long's translation, p. 35, XXXV

cx Ibid, p 20, XVI

cxi http://www.smithsonianmag.com/arts-culture/the-story-behind-banksy-4310304/

cxii Ibid

cxiii Long's translation, p. 36, XXXVII

cxiv Martin, George RR.
https://www.youtube.com/watch?v=7St9TtLzoLk
cxv Seneca, On the Shortness of Life, X,
http://www.forumromanum.org/literature/seneca_yo
unger/brev_e.html#10
cxvi Duckworth, p. 233
cxvii Seneca, On the Shortness of Life, X,
http://www.forumromanum.org/literature/seneca_yo
unger/brev_e.html#10
cxviii Meditations, 4:32
cxix Seneca, CDN Costa, On the Shortness of Life, pg.
4
cxx The Happy Life,
https://www.loebclassics.com/view/seneca_younger-
de_vita_beata/1932/pb_LCL254.107.xml
cxxi Ibid
cxxii Irvine, p. 129.
cxxiii

https://www.youtube.com/watch?v=Fw4Fg2Y4D2U
&feature=youtu.be&t=24m

cxxiv Holiday,
https://www.goodreads.com/work/quotes/26493723-
the-obstacle-is-the-way-the-timeless-art-of-turning-
adversity-to-advant?page=3
cxxv http://www.businessinsider.com/jim-rohn-youre-
the-average-of-the-five-people-you-spend-the-most-
time-with-2012-7
cxxvi Duckworth, Grit, p. 84.
cxxvii Irvine, p. 127
cxxviii Meditations, II.1s

cxxix Irvine, pg. 128, citing Marcus Aurelius, V.16, VI.44

cxxx Guide to the Good Life, p. 66

cxxxi

https://yogastories.wordpress.com/2010/09/17/fish-and-rice-a-story-about-self-control-and-gratitude-for-children-age-6-10-years/

cxxxii http://prokopton.com/2016/02/the-transformative-power-of-stoic-gratitude/

cxxxiii Ibid.

cxxxiv Watkins, Woodard, Stone, and Kolts, "Gratitude and Happiness: Development of a Measure of Gratitude and Relationships with Subjective Well-Being," Social Behavior and Personality Journal, 2003, p. 431.

cxxxv Ibid, p. 448

cxxxvi Ibid, p. 449

cxxxvii Guide to the Good Life, p. 81

Made in the USA
San Bernardino, CA
10 June 2018